Prentice Hall
Human Sexuality

Prentice Hall
Health

Pruitt, Allegrante,
Prothrow-Stith

PEARSON

Prentice Hall

Boston, Massachusetts
Upper Saddle River, New Jersey

Prentice Hall
Human Sexuality

Acknowledgments appear on p. 120, which constitutes an extension of this copyright page.

ISBN 0-13-190452-3
7 8 9 10 11   13 12 11 10 09

Program Authors

B. E. Pruitt

B. E. Pruitt, Ed.D., is Professor of Health Education at Texas A&M University. He served as executive director of the American Association for Health Education, and was the editor of the *American Journal of Health Education*. He has received numerous professional honors, including two National Professional Service Awards and the "Scholar" Award from the American Association for Health Education.

John P. Allegrante

John P. Allegrante, Ph.D., is Professor of Health Education at Teachers College and the Mailman School of Public Health at Columbia University in the City of New York. He is a past president and Distinguished Fellow of the Society for Public Health Education. He received the Distinguished Career Award in Public Health Education and Health Promotion from the American Public Health Association.

Deborah Prothrow-Stith

Deborah Prothrow-Stith, M.D., is Associate Dean, Professor and founder of the Division of Practice at Harvard School of Public Health. As former Massachusetts Public Health Commissioner, she expanded HIV and substance abuse services. She is nationally recognized for her leadership in addressing violence as a public health problem and for her books *Murder Is No Accident* and *Sugar and Spice and No Longer Nice*.

Content Reviewers

Eric R. Buhi, Ph.D.
University of South Florida
Tampa, Florida

Elizabeth Coolidge-Stolz, M.D.
North Reading, Massachusetts

Jena Nicols Curtis, Ed.D.
State University of New York
College at Cortland
Cortland, New York

James P. Marshall, Ph.D.
University of Arkansas
Little Rock, Arkansas

Lisa M. Romero, Dr. P. H.
Centers for Disease Control
and Prevention
Atlanta, Georgia

Health Educator Reviewers

Mike Code
Highlands High School
Fort Thomas, Kentucky

Elizabeth J. Godwin
Cape Coral High School
Cape Coral, Florida

Darrel Lang, Ed.D.
HIV/AIDS and Human Sexuality Consultant
Kansas State Department of Education
Topeka, Kansas

Kathleen St. Laurent, R.N., M.S.N.
Coyle and Cassidy High School
Taunton, Massachusetts

Cristina Thyron
Prairie High School
Vancouver, Washington

Contents

1

Understanding Sexuality

Go Online
PHSchool.com

Discovery EDUCATION™

TEENS Talk

CLASSROOM VIDEO #20

Pictures of "Perfection"

What's Important to You?

Complete this activity before you watch the video.

1. Rank the following qualities by how important you think they are to *your* overall attractiveness (with 1 being most important).
   _____ body shape
   _____ facial features
   _____ mature appearance
   _____ personality
   _____ intelligence
2. Now rank the list by how important you think each quality is to *other* people's attractiveness. How do your two rankings differ?
3. Now reflect. Do you think that your rankings for yourself and others are as they *should* be? Explain. **WRITING**

What Is Sexuality?

Objectives

▶ **Identify** how sexuality influences your personality and behavior.

▶ **Summarize** two areas of development significant to sexuality during the teen years.

▶ **List** four factors that influence sexuality.

▶ **Describe** how sexuality is expressed in everyday life.

Vocabulary

• sexuality
• gender
• gender role

Warm-Up

Myth I don't need to know about sexuality since I'm not sexually active.

Fact Sexuality is an integral part of who you are and how you behave, regardless of sexual experience.

WRITING What other myths do you think teens have about sexuality? What answers to the questions you have about sexuality do you hope this book will provide?

Defining Sexuality

As a teen, you are growing—physically, emotionally, mentally, socially, and creatively. And you are becoming more aware of your **sexuality**—everything about you that relates to, reflects, or expresses maleness or femaleness. Sexuality is influenced in large part by your sex—that is, being male or female in the biological sense. It is also influenced by your concepts of gender. **Gender** refers to the way people perceive maleness and femaleness to be defined by society.

Your sexuality influences how you think, how you feel about yourself and others, and how you behave. Remember that you do not need a boyfriend or girlfriend, nor to be sexually active, to express your sexuality. The way you dress and move, the gestures and facial expressions you use, the distance you stand from the person you are talking with, and other forms of body language convey your sexuality. What you say and how you say it can also reflect your sexuality. Talking comfortably about your body and your feelings, for example, is a positive expression of sexuality.

As a teen, you will experience significant changes in your awareness and expression of your sexuality. These are normal developments, but they may cause you to worry about your appearance, your feelings, and your behavior. Learning about your sexuality will help you to deal with these changes in a more confident way.

Factors Affecting Sexuality

Your sexuality develops and changes as you mature. **Four factors that influence sexuality are family, the media, peers, and adult role models.**

Influence of Family   The development of your sexuality begins when you are an infant. The touch of your parents, the warmth of your mother's body, and the sights and sounds that you experience all contribute to your awareness of your body as an infant. As you grow older, your parents serve as your first models of sexuality. When parents express physical affection with a hug or a kiss, children learn how their bodies can be used to express feelings in positive, healthy ways.

Parents also influence a child's understanding of gender roles. **Gender roles** are the behaviors and attitudes that are socially accepted as either masculine or feminine. These roles often are defined differently in different cultures. In fact, over time, they can change significantly within a culture. In the United States, gender roles have become less rigid in the last few decades.

Through their words and actions, parents display certain attitudes about gender roles in the family and as members of a community. For example, parents may share in household tasks and show respect for each other's work. By doing this, they foster the attitude that every person is of equal value and deserves respect.

Connect to YOUR LIFE   Describe one influence on how you view gender roles.

FIGURE 1   Gender roles are influenced by social interactions that begin soon after birth and continue throughout childhood.

Go Online
—HEALTH
LINKS℠

For: Updates on building a healthy body image
Visit: www.SciLinks.org/health
Web Code: ctn-1011

Influence of the Media Much of what you see, hear, and read in the media—television, music, movies, magazines, and newspapers— conveys messages about sexuality. These media messages may contradict what you have learned from your family. Keep in mind that the media try to entertain or sell things to their customers. To do this, they often use themes that appeal to people's anxieties, concerns, or hopes about their own sexuality. For example, many teenagers are self-conscious about their appearance. Advertisers may exploit these concerns by suggesting that people need to use their products or services to be sexually appealing.

To attract audiences, some television programs and movies deal with topics that involve sexual behavior. The serious risks of sexual behavior— such as unplanned pregnancy and sexually transmitted infections—are dealt with on some shows, but more often than not, they are ignored.

The lyrics of many pop songs also have a sexual theme. Unfortunately, some of these songs do not present a responsible message. For example, some songs treat women as objects or even glorify sexual violence.

Although you can receive negative messages and misinformation from the various media, you also can receive positive messages. For example, some movies, radio and television programs, and written articles inform you and increase your awareness and understanding of sexuality.

Connect to YOUR LIFE Which pop artists do you think portray sexuality in a responsible way? Explain.

FIGURE 2 Popular music presents many messages about sexuality. **Predicting** How do you think song lyrics might influence teen behavior?

MEDIA Wise

TV and Sexual Messages

How do your favorite TV shows portray teens? Are the teen characters better dressed, more beautiful, and more sex-savvy than students at your school? What kinds of messages about sex and sexuality are these fictional teens sending?

Do the teens act in responsible ways?	**Yes** **No**
Do the teens have serious discussions with adult role models about sex?	**Yes** **No**
Are the negative consequences of teen sex portrayed realistically?	**Yes** **No**
Do any of the characters who have been sexually active later choose to be abstinent?	**Yes** **No**

"Yes" answers represent more responsible messages about teen sex than "No" answers.

Activity Watch three TV shows that feature teens. For each show, use the checklist to evaluate each show's message about teens and sex. How did the shows compare? Which had the healthiest message for its viewers? Summarize your findings in a short essay.

Influence of Peers   Your peers also influence the development of your sexuality. For example, many teenagers find it comforting to have a close friend to talk with about their latest crush, or to ask for advice about fashion, hair styles, and personal care products. Friends who have a healthy attitude about their own sexuality help to shape positive attitudes about sexuality in others.

Some teens judge their own expressions of sexuality against their perceptions of peer "norms." Perceptions of peer norms—those behaviors teens think are typically practiced by their peers—may not lead to healthy decisions. For example, some teens think that most of their peers are sexually active. Even though this perception is usually inaccurate, teens may feel pressure to become sexually active themselves, before they are ready.

Influence of Adult Role Models   When you require reliable information about sexuality, to whom do you turn? In addition to talking to your parents, you may consult other family members, teachers, health professionals, clergy members, or other responsible adults. Even among well-informed adults, however, opinions about certain aspects of sexuality may vary greatly. It will be up to you to sort through the information you receive and to act responsibly.

FIGURE 3 By sitting close and sharing a joke, these teens are expressing their sexuality without even thinking about it.

Expressing Sexuality

Because sexuality is part of your personality, it is expressed in many of the things you do. The typical, everyday expressions of sexuality through dress, body language, and conversation usually happen on a subconscious level. Since they are so much a part of you, you tend not to think about them.

While you do not need to hide your sexual development, you do need to realize that calling attention to it with clothing or behavior may encourage situations you are not ready for. Similarly, you should not pretend an interest in someone if you do not feel it, and you should not be ashamed of these feelings if you have them.

Expressing sexuality to someone you consider special, on the other hand, involves a conscious effort to show your attraction and affection for that person. Sitting close, holding hands, and showing concern are all ways of expressing attraction and affection.

Often, two people in a relationship have different ideas about how they want to express their sexuality in a physical sense. They may disagree about how intimate they want to become. They may even feel different ways at different times. Whatever your feelings, you never owe anyone a more intimate sexual expression than you are comfortable with. You also should not pressure others to go farther in expressing their sexuality than is comfortable for them.

Section 1 Review

Key Ideas and Vocabulary

1. What is **sexuality?** How is it different from sexual activity?

2. What are **gender roles?**

3. How does sexuality change during the teen years?

4. List four factors that influence individual concepts of sexuality.

5. Give three examples of everyday expressions of sexuality.

Critical Thinking

6. **Applying Concepts** Give an example of one factor at your school that influences gender roles.

Health and Community

Media Messages Choose two or three magazine pictures that you think present messages about sexuality. Attach them to a sheet of paper and ask several teens and adults of both sexes to describe the sexual messages. Summarize their views. How do their views compare with your original views? **WRITING**

7. **Making Judgments** How do you think the factor you named in Question 6 affects students' concepts of sexuality? Explain.

8. **Relating Cause and Effect** Many teens think that more of their peers are sexually active than actually are. What are some of the reasons that teens might think this?

Concerns of Adolescence

Objectives

▶ **Identify** the physical changes related to sexuality that occur during puberty.

▶ **List** three factors that affect self-concept during adolescence.

Vocabulary

- adolescence
- puberty
- reproductive maturity
- secondary sex characteristics
- self-concept
- body image
- sexual awakening
- heterosexual
- homosexual
- bisexual

Warm-Up

Dear Advice Line,

I'm very self-conscious because I look more grown up than all of my friends. I'm tired of people staring at me and making comments about my body. What can I do?

WRITING What advice and reassurances would you offer this teen?

Changes in Your Body

If you were to compare a recent photograph of yourself to one taken three years ago, you would notice many changes. From about the ages of 12 to 19, you gradually change from a child into an adult. This period of gradual change is called **adolescence.** During adolescence, a person experiences many physical, mental, and emotional changes.

As photographs reveal, adolescence is a period of rapid physical growth. However, photos show only some of the changes taking place in your body. Important changes related to your sexuality are also happening. **During adolescence, the reproductive system matures and adult features appear. The timing of these changes varies greatly from person to person.**

The period of sexual development when a person becomes sexually mature and able to reproduce is known as **puberty.** Puberty usually begins before you reach adolescence and ends during mid-adolescence. You may have heard the term *puberty* used in many different ways. Some people use the term to refer to all of the changes of adolescence. However, the term refers specifically to the changes that happen to your reproductive system.

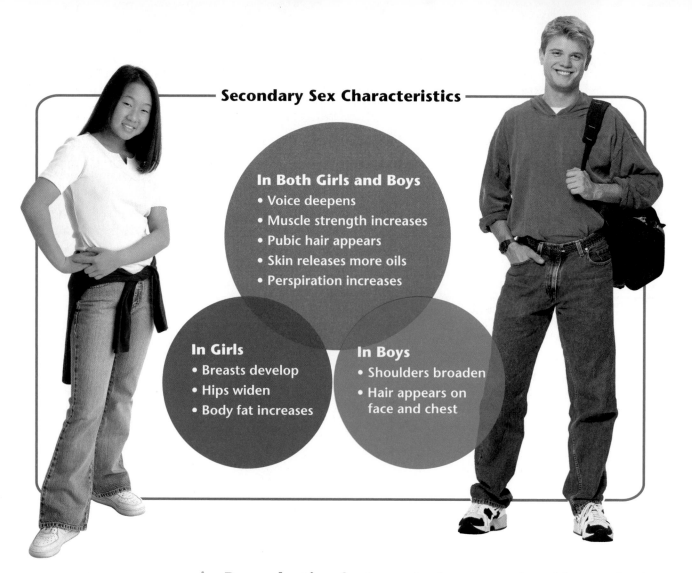

Secondary Sex Characteristics

In Both Girls and Boys
- Voice deepens
- Muscle strength increases
- Pubic hair appears
- Skin releases more oils
- Perspiration increases

In Girls
- Breasts develop
- Hips widen
- Body fat increases

In Boys
- Shoulders broaden
- Hair appears on face and chest

FIGURE 4 At puberty, sex hormones cause the development of secondary sex characteristics.

Reproductive System Sex hormones released from endocrine glands control the changes that occur during puberty. At some point between the ages of 9 and 16, the pituitary gland in the brain signals a girl's ovaries or a boy's testes to begin producing sex hormones. The ovaries produce eggs and the hormones estrogen and progesterone. The testes produce sperm and the hormone testosterone. You will learn more about the male and female reproductive systems in Chapter 2.

The release of sex hormones causes girls to begin to ovulate—to release eggs—and to menstruate. It causes boys to begin to produce sperm. Ovulation in girls and sperm production in boys signal **reproductive maturity,** or the ability to produce children.

Early in puberty, the body does not produce sex hormones consistently. In girls, this affects the regularity of the menstrual cycle. Many girls begin to ovulate before their menstrual cycles become regular. In fact, in some girls, menstrual cycles do not become regular for many years.

Appearance The sex hormones also cause the development of **secondary sex characteristics,** which are physical changes that develop during puberty, but are not directly involved in reproduction. Secondary sex characteristics are listed in Figure 4.

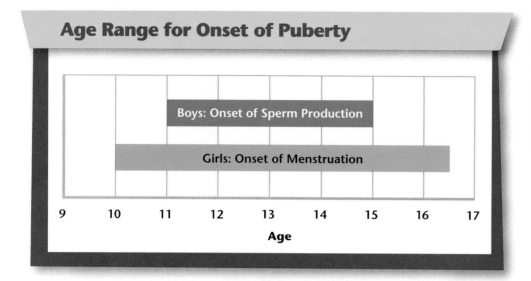

Age Range for Onset of Puberty

Boys: Onset of Sperm Production

Girls: Onset of Menstruation

Age

9   10   11   12   13   14   15   16   17

FIGURE 5 There is no "typical" age at which puberty begins. This timeline shows that the age range for onset of puberty is wide. **Calculating** What is the range in years between the earliest and latest onset of menstruation in girls? **MATH**

Early Bloomers and Late Bloomers If you are like most adolescents, you have probably compared your own physical development to that of your peers. Some of your classmates may already look like adults, while others may be just starting to show signs of puberty. You can see in Figure 5 that the age range for the "normal" onset of puberty is wide. Some people start puberty before middle school, some people start puberty toward the end of high school, and others start puberty somewhere in between.

Adolescents who develop at an early age, before most other adolescents, are sometimes called early bloomers. Those who develop at a later age, after most other adolescents, are called late bloomers. Although they may not think so, most early bloomers and late bloomers are developing at a normal rate.

What accounts for the wide range of ages at which puberty and the growth spurt begin? The ages at which people mature sexually and grow to their adult height are determined in large part by heredity. You are probably maturing at about the same age and speed as your parents did. Another factor that influences your unique timetable of development is your overall state of health.

 Connect to YOUR LIFE Do you consider yourself an early bloomer, late bloomer, or somewhere in between? Why?

Adjusting to Change The physical changes at puberty can be overwhelming at times. Some adolescents have difficulty adjusting to their changing body shape, and some are embarrassed or confused about the sexual changes occurring to their bodies. Having someone to talk to, especially a trusted adult, can help adolescents understand the changes and accept their feelings.

Go Online PHSchool.com

For: More on adolescence
Visit: PHSchool.com
Web Code: ctd-6201

Understanding Sexuality **11**

FIGURE 6 Developing a healthy self-concept means accepting yourself and being comfortable around others.

Accepting Yourself

Although puberty may bring physical changes before you feel prepared for them, it is a normal process that every teen experiences. Adjusting to these changes will affect your **self-concept**—that is, what you think of yourself, physically and mentally. Your self-concept will change during adolescence and continue to develop into adulthood. **Three factors that affect your self-concept are body image, emotions, and sexual feelings.**

Body Image   The way you see your physical self, your **body image,** is an important part of your self-concept. Some changes you now see may please you, and you may emphasize them with clothing, make-up, or regular workouts at the gym. Other changes may cause you some grief, and you may try to hide or change them. If you are unhappy with your body image, try to focus on your strengths and appreciate your unique physical appearance.

Emotions   The hormones that influence the physical changes of puberty also affect emotions. Changing levels of these hormones may create mood swings that can range from feelings of high energy and joy to feelings of exhaustion and depression. Flashes of anger, often for no apparent reason, are typical of the mood changes that accompany puberty. So is feeling "both ways at once"—for example, when you look forward to, yet dread, a school dance or simultaneously love and hate a parent or sibling.

The strong and sometimes conflicting emotions of adolescence can be confusing and stressful. It may help to ease your anxieties if you realize that everyone experiences these same problems to some degree during the natural process of becoming an adult.

Sexual Awakening Many of the concerns about body image and emotions that teenagers experience are related to another aspect of puberty—an increased awareness of, and sexual attraction to, other people. These feelings of sexual attraction are sometimes referred to as **sexual awakening.** It is only natural that you want to appear physically attractive to people to whom you are sexually attracted.

Your first feelings of sexual attraction may involve someone you have always known but now like in a different way. Or, you may find yourself attracted to someone new, or to your fantasy of the perfect date or ideal mate. Sometimes it may seem as though you are sexually attracted to everyone or as though you will never be interested in anyone. Just as the rate of physical development varies from person to person, so does the age at which teenagers experience sexual awakening.

Sexual Orientation As people mature sexually, they begin to establish their sexual orientation, or sexual preference. Most people are **heterosexual** (het uh roh SEK shoo ul)—as adults they are attracted to people of the opposite sex. Some people are **homosexual** (hoh moh SEK shoo ul)—as adults they are attracted to members of their own sex. Adults who are attracted to members of both sexes are called **bisexual.**

It is not unusual for young adolescents to prefer friends of their own sex, to have same-sex crushes on older friends, or even to have some sexual attraction to members of their own sex. This does not mean that they are or will be homosexual or bisexual. In many cases, this is just a part of the process of working through and establishing sexual orientation. Whatever a person's sexual orientation, it is a natural part of his or her own sexuality. It is not known what factors ultimately determine a person's sexual orientation.

Section 2 Review

Key Ideas and Vocabulary

1. What are two kinds of physical change at puberty that relate to sexuality?
2. List two **secondary sex characteristics** that develop in both boys and girls during adolescence.
3. What are three factors that affect self-concept during adolescence?
4. What is **sexual awakening?**

Critical Thinking

5. Comparing and Contrasting What event signals reproductive maturity in females? In males?

Health at Home

Self-Concept Evaluation Write down three things you like about yourself, three things you do routinely that you feel good about, and three tasks that were difficult for you to do but that you accomplished. Explain why each thing is important to your self-concept.

6. Making Judgments Do you think it is more difficult to be an early bloomer or a late bloomer? Why?
7. Applying Concepts How can having a healthy body image help a person accept the changes of adolescence? Explain.

Values and Responsibilities

Objectives

▶ **Identify** some of the serious consequences of sexual activity during adolescence.

▶ **Evaluate** how respecting individual differences and opinions can strengthen your self-concept.

Vocabulary

• value

Warm-Up

Quick Quiz In your private journal, rank the following values in order of their importance to you, from 1 (most important) to a 4 (least important). If two things seem of equal importance, you can give them the same number.

_____ My health

_____ My family's respect

_____ Self-respect

_____ Acceptance by my peers

WRITING How might your values affect your decisions about sexual activity? Are your actions consistent with your values? Would you like to re-examine either your decisions or your values? Explain.

What Are Your Values?

Greater freedom, greater independence, and greater responsibility—these are some of the things to expect during adolescence. But it's not always easy. While at times your parents may expect you to behave like an adult, at other times, you may feel they still treat you like a child. Sometimes, you may be furious about not being allowed to decide things for yourself. At other times, you may want someone to make the hard decisions for you.

Fortunately, as your world expands during adolescence, so does your ability to deal with it. You are learning to think ahead and to plan, to put yourself in someone else's place, to analyze, to predict consequences, and to see the many sides of an issue. With this new emotional and intellectual maturity, you become aware of your values. **Values** are the standards and beliefs that you consider important and that help you decide what is right and wrong. You have learned many of your values from your parents, guardians, other adults, religion, culture, and certain life experiences. Whatever your values, they act as guidelines for the decisions you are facing now and will face in the future.

Connect to YOUR LIFE What people or experiences do you think have influenced your values the most?

Values and Sexual Decision-Making   When facing an important decision, it is wise to examine your feelings and wishes in light of your values. Among the many decisions you may make in adolescence and as an adult are those involving the expression of your sexuality. The strong feelings that accompany your sexual development in adolescence are likely to lead to relationships that are based on mutual sexual attraction. The quiz at the beginning of this section helped you to identify how your values will affect your decision-making in such relationships. For example, suppose you value your family's respect the most, and they disapprove of sex before marriage. This knowledge will help you stick to your decision to be abstinent.

When sexual feelings are strong, it may be difficult to abstain from sexual activity, but it is well worth it. **Sexual activity can have serious consequences, including sexually transmitted infections and HIV, pregnancy, and negative effects on your relationships and self-esteem.** You will learn more about sexual decision-making and about skills for practicing sexual abstinence in Chapter 3.

Talking Things Over   Making decisions about relationships and sexual activity can be difficult, even when you feel quite sure of your values. Sometimes, it is helpful to talk things over with a responsible adult just to get another perspective on a difficult situation. Try to begin your discussion with your parents, even if you are embarrassed. Their concern for you often can help you overcome embarrassment, disappointment, disagreements, or even anger. Additional help may be available from teachers, health professionals, members of the clergy, and counselors. It is not shameful to ask for guidance. To know you need help and to ask for and accept it is a sign of maturity.

FIGURE 7   Talking to a parent about sexual matters may be difficult, but can help you clarify your values and make good decisions.

"I don't feel ready for sex, but it's all that my friends talk about."

"Don't worry about what your friends think. It's important to be true to yourself."

FIGURE 8 By accepting your individuality and that of others, the pressure to conform to what you perceive as "normal" will ease.

Appreciating Differences

You know, of course, that everyone, including yourself, is different from everyone else. Everyone has his or her unique physical, mental, and sexual traits. Everyone has a unique personality. During adolescence, these differences often become more pronounced. At the same time, the pressure to conform—to be like everyone else—is especially strong. No one wants to seem particularly different. If, however, you accept your individuality and that of others, this pressure to conform eases.

Trying to see things from other people's points of view can strengthen your own self-concept. This means trying to be open to others' opinions. It means respecting each person's right to be what they are, even if you happen to be something quite different. It also means not pressuring people to go against their values just to be a part of your crowd. Accepting others will help you be comfortable with the ways you feel different from your peers. And it will help you feel more confident in making the decisions that are best for you.

Section 3 Review

Key Ideas and Vocabulary

1. What are **values?** Name three factors that can influence a person's values.

2. List three risks of sexual activity.

3. Explain how an appreciation of other points of view can strengthen self-concept.

Critical Thinking

4. Making Judgments Why are values important?

Health at School

Promoting Respect Work with a small group of your classmates to produce a poster that promotes respect for all students. Arrange with your teacher to display your poster in a school hallway or assembly room.

5. Applying Concepts How are values and sexual decision-making related?

TEENS Talk

Pictures of "Perfection" How did the video change your perception of models? Of yourself?

Reviewing Key Ideas

Section 1

1. Sexuality is best described as
   a. behavior involving sexual activity.
   b. something that causes pregnancy.
   c. expressions of sexual attraction.
   d. expressions of maleness or femaleness.

2. Which of the following affects teens' concepts of sexuality?
   a. childhood experiences
   b. movies and TV
   c. friends
   d. all of the above

3. How are sexuality and sexual activity related?

4. What are some ways in which parents influence their children's sexuality?

5. **Critical Thinking** How do popular media influence teen sexuality? Do you think the media's influence has a mostly positive or mostly negative effect on teen sexuality? Explain.

6. **Critical Thinking** How do culturally defined gender roles affect expressions of sexuality? Explain using two examples.

Section 2

7. Puberty
   a. is all the changes of adolescence.
   b. lasts longer than adolescence.
   c. is controlled by sex hormones.
   d. is more stressful for boys than for girls.

8. Which of the following is a secondary sex characteristic?
   a. reproductive maturity
   b. sperm production
   c. increase in perspiration
   d. increase in height

9. How does puberty affect a person's sexuality?

10. Describe a typical "mood swing" that a teen might experience.

11. What is sexual orientation? Define three kinds of sexual orientation.

12. **Critical Thinking** How do you think ads for acne cures on TV affect teen body image? Explain.

Section 3

13. Beliefs that help you decide between right and wrong are called
    a. gender roles.   b. opinions.
    c. values.   d. self-concepts.

14. What values have you learned from your parents?

15. Why is it helpful to talk to a trusted adult about sex and sexuality?

16. **Critical Thinking** How would you describe to a young child what the term *values* means?

Building Health Skills

17. **Analyzing Influences** Your younger sister's friends are telling her to stop spending time at math club and start paying more attention to looking sexy. What is the message that she is getting about her sexuality? What advice would you give her? **WRITING**

18. **Advocacy** Your friend is wondering if he might be homosexual. Some of his old friends have started to avoid him and he is feeling depressed. How can you help? What other support would you recommend he seek out?

19. **Making Decisions** Suppose your "popular" friends spend a lot of their time making unkind comments about other teens who aren't part of their crowd. This makes you uncomfortable. What would you do?

Health and Community

Gender Roles In a small group, brainstorm a list of negative gender stereotypes that affect males and females. Discuss how these stereotypes limit both sexes from reaching their full potential. What gender stereotypes in your community would you like to see change? Write and perform a skit that shows what an "alternative" world without the stereotype would be like.

The Reproductive System

Go Online
PHSchool.com

![Discovery Education logo]

TEENS Talk

CLASSROOM VIDEO #24

Taking Charge of Your Health

Preview Activity

Where Do You Get Your Health Information?

Complete this activity before you watch the video.

1. Choose a health topic you would like to know more about.
2. Write down a list of different sources that could provide you with more information on that topic. **WRITING**
3. Rank the sources you listed from most reliable to least reliable.
4. When you have looked for health information in the past, did you go to the most reliable source? Why or why not?

The Male Reproductive System

Objectives

▶ **Describe** three functions of the male reproductive system.

▶ **Identify** five ways to keep the male reproductive system healthy.

Vocabulary

- sperm
- fertilization
- testes
- testosterone
- scrotum
- penis
- semen
- ejaculation
- erection
- orgasm
- nocturnal emission
- masturbation
- testicular torsion
- infertility

Warm-Up

Myth Cancers of the male reproductive system only affect older men.

Fact Cancer of the testis (testicular cancer) is most common in teens and young men, not older men.

WRITING Why do you think that people have a number of misconceptions about the reproductive system?

Structure and Function

One essential function of all living things is reproduction, the process by which organisms produce offspring. In humans, the process begins with the development of reproductive cells in the bodies of males and females. In males, the reproductive cells are called **sperm. The functions of the male reproductive system are to produce sex hormones, to produce and store sperm, and to deliver sperm to the female reproductive system.** There, a sperm cell may join with an egg in a process called **fertilization.** Under the right conditions, a fertilized egg develops into a baby.

Testes Look at Figure 1 to see the organs of the male reproductive system. Locate the two oval-shaped **testes** (TES teez), the male reproductive glands. The testes (singular, *testis*) have two major functions—the production of testosterone and the production of sperm. The sex hormone **testosterone** affects the production of sperm and signals certain physical changes at puberty, such as the growth of facial hair.

The testes, also called testicles, hang outside the main body cavity, within a sac of skin called the **scrotum.** Because they are located outside the body, the temperature of the testes is a few degrees lower than the temperature inside the body. Sperm need this lower temperature to develop properly and survive.

In some males, one or both of the testes may not descend into the scrotum before birth, a condition called undescended testis. Sperm will not develop properly in an undescended testis because the temperature is too high. The condition is also a risk factor for testicular cancer. Surgery is usually performed before age two to correct this condition.

Penis The **penis** is the external sexual organ through which sperm leave the body. The tip of the penis is covered with loose skin, called the foreskin. In some males the foreskin is removed shortly after birth. This surgical procedure is known as circumcision. The decision to circumcise an infant is usually based on cultural or religious reasons. Whether there is an overall health benefit to circumcision is still being debated.

Other Structures Besides the external structures, the male reproductive system also includes internal ducts and accessory glands. These structures, which are shown in Figure 1, play an important role in storing and releasing sperm.

Sperm Production Once a male reaches puberty, millions of sperm are produced in his testes each day. Sperm production begins when the hypothalamus signals the pituitary gland to release two hormones—luteinizing hormone (LH) and follicle-stimulating hormone (FSH). LH signals the testes to begin making testosterone. Testosterone and FSH then trigger the production of sperm. Sperm production continues throughout adulthood.

 Why do you think some people are uncomfortable using the proper terms for reproductive structures?

Male Reproductive System

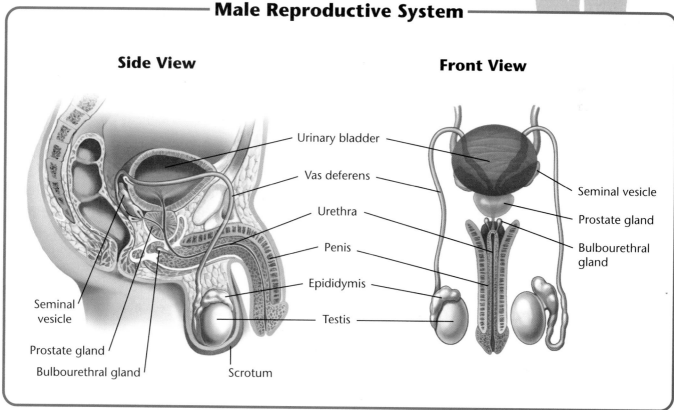

Side View

Front View

Urinary bladder

Vas deferens

Urethra

Penis

Epididymis

Testis

Seminal vesicle

Prostate gland

Bulbourethral gland

Scrotum

Seminal vesicle

Prostate gland

Bulbourethral gland

FIGURE 1 The male reproductive system produces, stores, and releases sperm.

The Pathway of Sperm

FIGURE 2 Sperm travel through the reproductive system before they are released. **Interpreting Diagrams** Where do sperm complete their maturation?

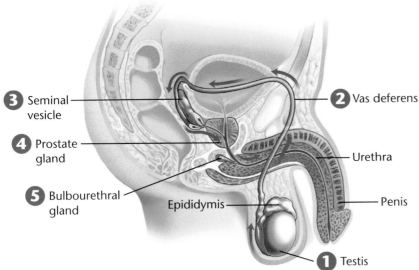

① Seminal vesicle

④ Prostate gland

⑤ Bulbourethral gland

Epididymis

② Vas deferens

Urethra

Penis

① Testis

① Sperm are produced in the **testes.** They mature and are stored in the **epididymis.**

② Sperm travel through the **vas deferens** to the seminal vesicles.

③ **Seminal vesicles** add a fluid that provides a source of energy for the active sperm.

④ The **prostate gland** adds a fluid that protects the sperm.

⑤ The **bulbourethral glands** add a fluid that protects sperm from acidic conditions in the **urethra.**

▲ **A sperm cell**

The Pathway of Sperm Look at Figure 2 to track the pathway of sperm through the male reproductive system. Note that during their passage through the male reproductive system, sperm cells mix with fluids produced by the prostate and two other glands. The mixture of sperm cells and these fluids is called **semen** (SEE mun).

Release of Sperm The ejection of semen from the penis is called **ejaculation.** Ejaculation occurs when the penis is in an erect state. During an **erection,** the penis becomes larger and stiffer as blood chambers in the penis become filled with blood.

Ejaculation occurs when the muscles in the male reproductive system and at the base of the bladder contract, forcing semen through the urethra. The urethra—a tube that passes through the penis to the outside of the body—carries urine as well as sperm, but not at the same time. Several million sperm cells are released during one ejaculation. Ejaculation is usually accompanied by **orgasm,** or sexual climax, which is marked by feelings of intense pleasure.

You learned that after a male reaches puberty, the testes produce millions of sperm daily. What happens if these sperm are not ejaculated? Sperm stored in the male reproductive system eventually degenerate, meaning they break down, and are disposed of.

Concerns at Puberty

Most boys have many questions and concerns about the changes that occur to their bodies during puberty.

Sexual Arousal One change that results from the rise in hormone levels is an increase in sexual feelings. Males have erections throughout their lives, from babyhood to old age. At puberty, however, a male may have erections more frequently, sometimes for no apparent reason. Such erections may sometimes be embarrassing, but they are normal.

During puberty, males may also notice that they are more sensitive to sexual stimulation. Sexual fantasies, being close to an attractive person, touching the penis or scrotum, wearing tight clothing, and even needing to urinate can all cause an erection. An erection does not need to result in ejaculation—in fact, most do not. The penis soon returns to its soft state.

Nocturnal Emissions It is also common for a teen male to experience a **nocturnal emission,** or "wet dream," which is ejaculation during sleep. Nocturnal emissions occur because sperm production during puberty causes an increased pressure in the reproductive system. Nocturnal emissions are normal and may occur frequently. It is also normal not to experience nocturnal emissions.

Masturbation Orgasm and ejaculation can also result from masturbation. **Masturbation** is the touching of one's own genitals for sexual pleasure. Some people once thought that masturbation could cause acne, mental illness, infertility, and other bad effects. This is not true. However, some people today still object to masturbation on moral or religious grounds. Most doctors agree that masturbation is harmless unless it becomes a preoccupation, makes you feel guilty, or interferes with your daily activities.

FIGURE 3 Changes at puberty can lead to concerns about your physical appearance. Remember that not all boys experience puberty the same way, or at the same age.

Physical Appearance It is also common for teen males to be concerned about their physical appearance. Many teen males, for example, worry about the size of their penis. Size depends on heredity and on the stage of puberty the male has reached. The eventual size of the penis has nothing to do with a male's ability to reproduce or to give a partner sexual pleasure. Furthermore, most erect penises are about the same size, no matter how large or small they are when they are not erect.

Breast enlargement is another thing that worries some teen males during puberty. About 40 percent of boys have some breast swelling or tenderness, especially early in puberty when hormone levels change rapidly. This condition usually reverses itself as hormone production becomes more constant. Any teen male who is concerned about breast enlargement should consult his doctor.

Go Online

HEALTH LINKS

For: Updates on male reproductive health
Visit: www.SciLinks.org/health
Web Code: ctn-6182

Keeping Healthy

A number of medical conditions can affect the male reproductive system. However, teens who adopt healthy habits can reduce their risk of problems. **Caring for the male reproductive system involves cleanliness, sexual abstinence, protection from trauma, self-exams, and regular medical checkups.**

Cleanliness   Healthy habits start with cleanliness. It is important to thoroughly clean the external organs—the penis and scrotum—daily, preferably during a shower or bath. Each day, an uncircumcised male should gently pull the foreskin back to clean the head of the penis. Drying the groin area well after showering can prevent fungal infections that cause jock itch.

Sexual Abstinence   A number of serious infections of the reproductive system and other body systems can result from sexual contact. Healthy choices regarding sexual behavior can prevent such infections. The only way to eliminate your risk of sexually transmitted infections is to abstain—or refrain from—sexual activity. In other words, practice sexual abstinence. Sexually transmitted infections will be discussed further in Chapter 5.

Protection From Trauma   Good health also requires protection and prevention. During athletic activities, males should wear a protector, also called a "cup," or supporter. Tight clothing should be avoided, since tight pants or underwear can irritate or cause pain in the groin area.

Males should also be careful when lifting heavy objects. Pressure in the abdomen during lifting can push a loop of intestine out of the abdominal cavity, causing a hernia. An inguinal (ING gwuh nul) hernia results if part of the intestine pushes into the scrotum. Surgery is almost always necessary to correct an inguinal hernia.

One of the most serious reproductive disorders that may affect male teens is testicular torsion. **Testicular torsion** is the twisting of a testis so that the blood vessels leading to the testis also twist, cutting off the blood supply. Testicular torsion can happen during strenuous exercise or even during sleep.

Testicular torsion is a medical emergency. If you ever have sudden pain or swelling of a testis, you must see a doctor *immediately*. The blood vessel has to be untwisted by a surgeon within about six hours to keep the testis alive.

FIGURE 4   This catcher protects himself with a helmet, face guard, body padding, and a "cup" that protects his reproductive organs from injury.

Self-Exams It is important for males to monitor their own bodies for any signs of possible medical problems. Pain when urinating, unusual discharges, or sores on the genitals require a medical examination. Such conditions should not be self-treated.

Males, especially teens and young men, should also examine their testes for signs of testicular cancer. Many testicular cancers occur in males in their teens and twenties. Testicular cancer is the most common type of cancer in males between 15 and 34 years of age. However, it can be cured if detected early and treated promptly. Most testicular cancers are first noticed by men themselves, not by their doctors.

Figure 5 outlines the procedure for the testicular self-exam. The best time to perform a self-exam is after a hot shower or bath, when the scrotum is relaxed and the testes can be felt more easily. The American Cancer Society recommends that teen males discuss with a doctor how often to perform self-exams.

Connect to YOUR LIFE Why is it important for males in their teens to know the symptoms of testicular cancer?

FIGURE 5 Males should follow this procedure to perform the testicular self-exam.
Comparing and Contrasting Where is the typical location of an abnormal lump compared with the location of the epididymis?

Testicular Self-Exam

① Examine each testis separately with both hands.

▶ Roll each testis between the thumbs and fingers of both hands.

▶ Look and feel for any hard lumps or smooth, rounded masses, or any change in the size, shape, or texture of the testes. If lumps are present, they are usually found in the front or sides of the testes.

▶ Learn to recognize what the epididymis feels like so you won't confuse it with a lump. The epididymis appears as a small "bump" on the back side of the testis, toward the back of the body.

② Report any abnormalities to your doctor immediately.

▶ Lumps may not be cancerous, but only a doctor can make a diagnosis.

▶ Other signs of testicular cancer are enlargement of a testis, dull aching in the genital area, or a feeling of heaviness in the scrotum. However, testicular cancer is not typically painful when it first develops.

Medical Checkups Medical exams throughout life can help ensure reproductive health. Teen males should expect a few differences in procedure from their childhood checkups. For example, the doctor will probably feel around your genitals to check for lumps or pain. The doctor may also ask you whether you have ejaculated, and whether you have any concerns about your sexual development. This is the time to bring up any worries you have or just to ask questions out of curiosity.

The prostate gland is of particular concern after middle age. In many older men, the prostate becomes enlarged or develops cancer. An enlarged prostate does not necessarily indicate either disease or illness, but it can cause discomfort and frequent urination. An enlarged prostate may also make urination painful or difficult. If that happens, surgery is usually required.

Starting at age 50, men are encouraged to get screened for prostate cancer during their regular medical exams. After lung cancer, prostate cancer is the second most common cause of cancer death in men.

Another condition a doctor can diagnose is **infertility,** the condition of being unable to reproduce. Infertility can affect both males and females. In males, infertility is marked by the inability to produce healthy sperm or the production of too few sperm. Three causes of infertility are exposure to certain chemicals, having mumps after puberty, and having an undescended testis.

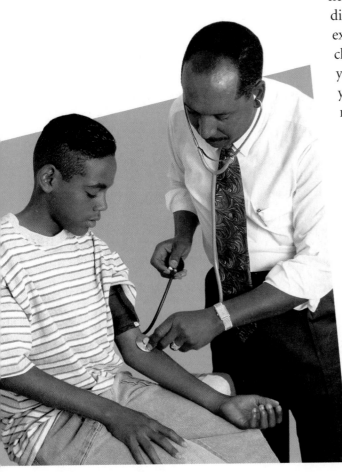

FIGURE 6 Your doctor can answer any questions you have about your reproductive health.

Section 1 Review

Key Ideas and Vocabulary

1. What are three main functions of the male reproductive system?
2. What is the name of the sac in which the **testes** are located?
3. What is **semen**, and how is it formed?
4. List five things that males should do to maintain reproductive health.
5. What are two kinds of problems with sperm that can lead to **infertility** in males?

Health at Home

Reminder Card Write an e-mail to a male family member reminding him of the importance of regular medical checkups and self-exams. **WRITING**

Critical Thinking

6. **Sequencing** Arrange the following structures in the order in which sperm pass by or travel through them: epididymis; vas deferens; testes; prostate gland; seminal vesicles
7. **Applying Concepts** How could more young men be convinced to follow the recommendations for reproductive health? **WRITING**

The Female Reproductive System

Objectives

▶ **Describe** three functions of the female reproductive system.

▶ **Summarize** the stages of the menstrual cycle.

▶ **Identify** five ways to keep the female reproductive system healthy.

Vocabulary

- ova
- ovaries
- estrogen
- progesterone
- ovulation
- fallopian tubes
- uterus
- vagina
- hymen
- menstrual cycle
- menopause
- vaginitis
- cystitis
- Pap smear
- mammogram

Warm-Up

Dear Advice Line,
I've been going to the same male doctor since I was a little kid. My doctor is really nice, but since my body started developing, I just don't feel comfortable having my checkups with him anymore. I'd like to see a female doctor. Is it OK to feel this way? What should I do?

WRITING Do you think this girl's feelings are normal? Write back with your advice.

Structure and Function

You learned that the reproductive cells in males are called sperm. In females, they are called eggs, or **ova** (singular, *ovum*). **The functions of the female reproductive system are to produce sex hormones, to produce eggs, and to provide a nourishing environment in which a fertilized egg can develop into a baby.**

Ovaries   Look at Figure 7 on page 28 to see the organs of the female reproductive system. The reproductive glands in which eggs are produced are called **ovaries.** The ovaries are located a few inches below the waist, one on each side of the body. Each ovary is about the size of an almond. The ovaries have two important functions: they produce the female sex hormones estrogen and progesterone, and they release mature egg cells. The sex hormone **estrogen** activates certain physical changes at puberty, such as breast development, and controls the maturation of eggs. **Progesterone** activates changes to a woman's reproductive system before and during pregnancy.

When a girl is born, each ovary contains hundreds of thousands of immature eggs. The eggs begin to mature, or ripen, when the girl reaches puberty. Once puberty begins, one of the ovaries releases a ripened egg about once every month in a process called **ovulation.** The tiny egg that is released is no larger than the period at the end of this sentence.

Fallopian Tubes   Figure 7 also shows the location of the two **fallopian tubes** (fuh LOH pee un)—passageways that carry eggs away from the ovaries. When the ovary releases an egg during ovulation, the fingerlike ends of the fallopian tube draw the egg into the tube. Eggs, unlike sperm, cannot swim. Tiny hairlike extensions called cilia line the fallopian tube and sweep the egg toward the uterus. If sperm are present around the egg, it may be fertilized. The fallopian tubes are where fertilization usually occurs.

Uterus   The **uterus** is a hollow, muscular, pear-shaped organ. In the uterus, a fertilized egg can develop and grow. The uterus has several layers of tissue and a rich supply of blood that protect and nourish the developing baby.

The narrow base of the uterus is called the cervix. When a baby is ready to be born, the cervix softens and expands to allow the baby to pass through to the vagina.

Vagina   The **vagina,** or birth canal, is a hollow, muscular passage leading from the uterus to the outside of the body. Sperm enter a female's body through the vagina. During childbirth, the baby passes out of the mother's body through the vagina. The walls of the vagina are very elastic, which allows it to expand dramatically during childbirth.

Connect to YOUR LIFE   **Where could you find reliable information about the female reproductive system?**

Female Reproductive System

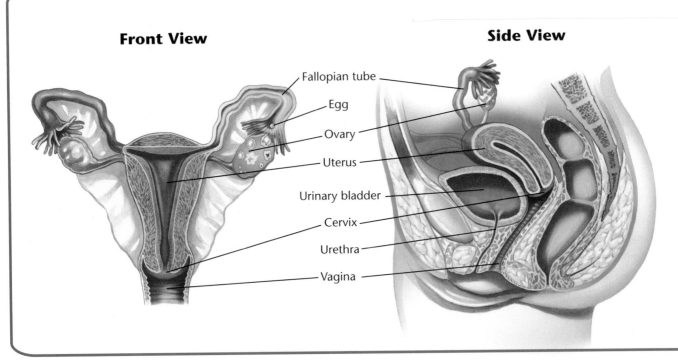

Front View

Side View

- Fallopian tube
- Egg
- Ovary
- Uterus
- Urinary bladder
- Cervix
- Urethra
- Vagina

External Organs   The locations of the external female reproductive organs are shown below. At the base of the abdomen on top of the pubic bone is a soft, fatty tissue known as the mons pubis (mahnz PYOO bis). At puberty, the mons pubis becomes covered with pubic hair.

Below the mons pubis and surrounding the vaginal opening are two folds of soft skin. The outer folds are known as the outer labia (LAY bee uh), or the labia majora. The outer labia are covered with pubic hair. The inner folds, known as the inner labia or the labia minora, contain many nerve endings and are sensitive to touch.

Another highly sensitive organ, the clitoris, is located within the inner labia. The clitoris plays a major role in female sexual arousal and contains many nerve endings and blood vessels.

In females, orgasm is marked by rhythmic contractions of the muscles of the vagina and pelvis. Not all females have orgasms. The lack of orgasm has no effect on the ability to reproduce. A female can become pregnant with or without orgasm.

Just below the clitoris is a small opening that leads to the urethra, the tube through which urine leaves the body. Unlike in the male, the urethra is not part of the female reproductive system. Below the urethral opening is the separate opening to the vagina.

The vaginal opening may be partly covered with a thin membrane known as the **hymen** (HY mun). The hymen usually has several openings in it, which allow for the passage of menstrual flow. The hymen may tear for various reasons, including vigorous exercise, tampon insertion, or sexual intercourse. Some girls are born without a hymen.

FIGURE 7   The female reproductive system produces eggs and provides a nourishing environment in which a fertilized egg can develop. **Interpreting Diagrams** Which organ releases mature eggs into the fallopian tube?

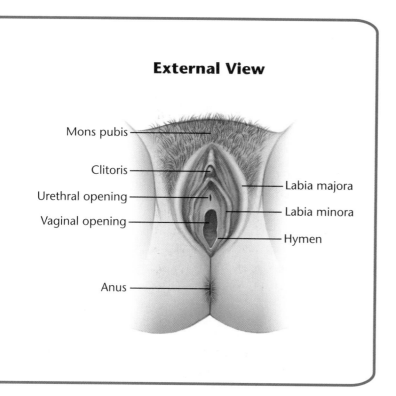

External View

Mons pubis

Clitoris

Urethral opening

Vaginal opening

Labia majora

Labia minora

Hymen

Anus

Concerns at Puberty

Most girls have many questions and concerns about the changes that occur to their bodies during puberty.

Sexual Arousal   Like most teen males, females also may notice an increase in sexual feelings during puberty. A photograph of a favorite movie star, a dream or fantasy, the presence of an attractive person, or some other stimulus may cause the heart to speed up and the breathing rate to quicken. Females may notice a feeling of wetness in and around the vagina, and may also have a swollen feeling in the pelvis. These are normal signs of sexual excitement.

Masturbation   Like males, some females masturbate, or touch their own genitals to obtain sexual pleasure. Some people object to masturbation on moral or religious grounds. Most doctors agree that masturbation is harmless unless it becomes a preoccupation, makes you feel guilty, or interferes with your daily activities.

Physical Appearance   One of the most common concerns of young women during puberty is breast development. In spite of what some girls believe, there is no "perfect" or "normal" breast size or shape. One breast may be a little larger than the other. The nipples may stick out or turn in. Breast size and appearance generally have no effect on the ability to feel sexual excitement or to nurse a child.

Just as breast size and shape vary from woman to woman, so does each girl's timetable for breast development. Some girls may notice breast development as early as age 8; others may not start developing until age 14 or later. It is quite normal for teen girls of the same age to be at different stages of breast development.

FIGURE 8   Teen girls, like boys, may worry about their physical appearance during puberty. Focusing on your strengths is one way to boost your self-confidence.

Sexuality in Music Videos

When watching your favorite music videos, you may not think about the hidden, or not-so-hidden, meanings they contain. What messages are conveyed about sex? Consider these questions as they relate to music videos.

1. Are there suggestive close-ups on body parts?   Yes   No

2. Is there non-verbal flirting (such as suggestive body positions or touching)?   Yes   No

3. Does anyone dress suggestively or take off any clothing?   Yes   No

4. Does anyone use force to touch or kiss someone?   Yes   No

5. Is there sexual bias—a greater emphasis on women's or men's bodies?   Yes   No

A "Yes" answer to one or more questions may indicate a video that presents sex in an unhealthy way.

Activity Think about how music videos make you feel about your body. In general, do they represent sex in a healthy or unhealthy way? Explain. **WRITING**

The Menstrual Cycle

As you learned, males typically produce millions of sperm cells every day after reaching puberty. Females, on the other hand, usually produce only one mature egg cell each month during a process called the **menstrual cycle** (MEN stroo ul). **During the menstrual cycle, an ovary releases a mature egg. The egg travels to the uterus. If the egg is not fertilized, the uterine lining is shed and a new cycle begins.**

Factors Affecting the Menstrual Cycle On average, a menstrual cycle lasts 28 days. However, cycles as short as 21 days or as long as 35 days can be normal for some individuals. The endocrine system controls the menstrual cycle. The hormones involved include FSH and LH, which are released by the pituitary gland, and estrogen and progesterone, which are released from the ovaries. Factors such as diet, stress, exercise, and weight gain or weight loss also affect the menstrual cycle. The menstrual cycle may be irregular at times, especially during puberty.

Except during pregnancy, menstrual cycles occur each month from puberty until about the age of 45 to 55. At that time of life, called **menopause,** the ovaries slow down their hormone production and no longer release mature eggs. Gradually, the menstrual cycle stops, and the woman is no longer able to become pregnant.

The Menstrual Cycle

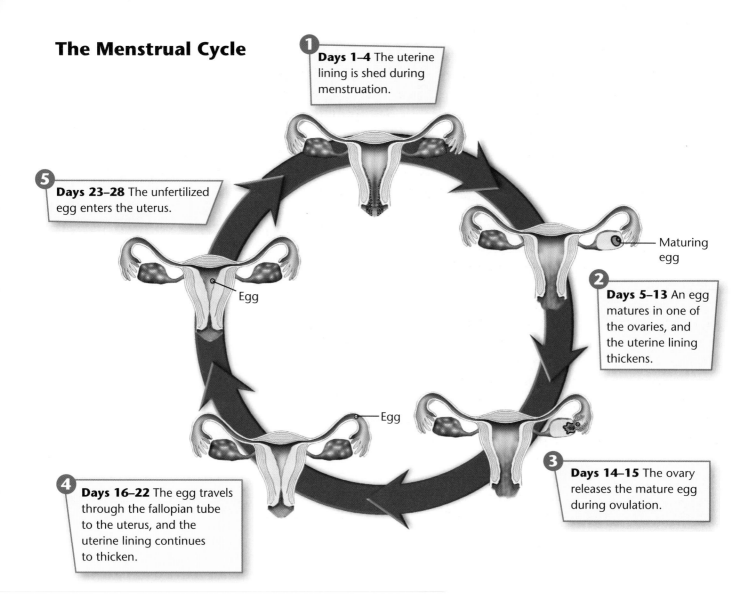

1 **Days 1–4** The uterine lining is shed during menstruation.

5 **Days 23–28** The unfertilized egg enters the uterus.

Egg

Maturing egg

2 **Days 5–13** An egg matures in one of the ovaries, and the uterine lining thickens.

Egg

3 **Days 14–15** The ovary releases the mature egg during ovulation.

4 **Days 16–22** The egg travels through the fallopian tube to the uterus, and the uterine lining continues to thicken.

FIGURE 9 The thickening of the lining of the uterus, ovulation, and menstruation are key events of the menstrual cycle.
Interpreting Diagrams
Through which structure does an egg travel before reaching the uterus?

Stages of the Menstrual Cycle   Follow the stages of a typical menstrual cycle in Figure 9. During the first half of the cycle, an egg matures inside one of the ovaries. Meanwhile, the lining of the uterus thickens. At about the middle of the cycle—typically on day 14— ovulation occurs. The mature egg is released by the ovary and travels into the fallopian tube. A female is most fertile, or able to become pregnant, around the time of ovulation.

It takes about seven days for the egg to travel through the fallopian tube into the uterus. During this time the uterine lining continues to thicken, and the blood supply to it increases. If the egg has not been fertilized by the time it reaches the uterus, the uterine lining breaks down.

The blood and tissue of the thickened lining pass out of the body through the vagina in a process called menstruation, or the menstrual period. As menstruation is taking place, another egg begins to mature in one of the ovaries. Thus menstruation marks the end of one cycle and the beginning of another. In general, a menstrual period lasts about 3 to 5 days. Most women wear either a sanitary pad or a tampon to absorb the menstrual flow.

Menstrual Discomfort During the menstrual period, some women may experience abdominal cramps or other discomfort. Cramps are caused by contractions of the uterus. See Figure 10 for some ways to relieve menstrual cramps. For severe cramps or for any other menstrual concerns, women should see a medical professional.

Some women experience discomfort some time before the menstrual period. This condition, known as premenstrual syndrome, or PMS, is marked by nervous tension, mood swings, headaches, bloating, and irritability. The dramatic change in hormone levels that occurs before menstruation begins may cause PMS. Some doctors recommend that PMS sufferers reduce their intake of salt, sugar, and caffeine, get regular exercise, and try other stress-reduction techniques.

Toxic Shock Syndrome A rare but serious medical condition associated with tampon use is toxic shock syndrome. This syndrome is caused by a bacterial infection. Symptoms of toxic shock syndrome include a sudden high fever, a rash, vomiting, diarrhea, and dizziness. Because toxic shock syndrome can lead to death, a woman with any of these symptoms during her period should seek medical attention immediately. To decrease the risk of toxic shock syndrome, women should use tampons with the lowest possible absorbency for their needs and change tampons often.

 Connect to YOUR LIFE What misconceptions did you hold about menstruation before reading this section?

Go Online PHSchool.com

For: More on the menstrual cycle
Visit: PHSchool.com
Web Code: ctd-6183

Menstrual cramps ? **Try this . . .**
• **Engage in moderate exercise.**
• **Take a warm bath.**
• **Apply a heating pad to the abdomen.**
• **Take aspirin or ibuprofen with doctor's approval.**

FIGURE 10 Following these simple tips can help relieve menstrual cramps.

FIGURE 11 Daily washing is an important part of keeping the reproductive system healthy.

Keeping Healthy

A number of medical conditions can affect the female reproductive system. Teens who adopt healthy habits can reduce their risk of problems. **Caring for the female reproductive system involves cleanliness, sexual abstinence, prompt treatment for infections, self-exams, and regular medical checkups.**

Cleanliness One important health habit is cleanliness, including daily washing of the external vaginal area. Cleanliness is especially important during menstruation, as is the regular changing of sanitary pads or tampons. Feminine hygiene sprays, douches, and deodorant tampons are not necessary. In fact, they may be harmful if they cover up signs of an infection or cause irritation. If washing does not get rid of normal body odors, or if any unusual discharge is noted, seek medical attention.

Sexual Abstinence A number of serious infections can result from sexual contact. Healthy choices regarding sexual behavior can prevent such infections. The only way to eliminate your risk of sexually transmitted infections is to abstain from sexual activity.

Prompt Treatment for Infections Some infections of the reproductive system are not related to sexual behavior. Many women experience **vaginitis,** a vaginal infection caused by yeast, bacteria, or other microorganisms. Symptoms can include an unusual discharge or odors, itching, and a burning sensation during urination. Only a doctor can diagnose the specific cause of vaginitis and provide appropriate treatment.

Another common problem among females is **cystitis** (sih STY tis), an infection of the bladder. Cystitis is caused by bacteria that travel up the urethra into the bladder. Symptoms include the urge to urinate frequently and a burning sensation during urination. If you experience these symptoms, you should consult a doctor. If left untreated, cystitis can lead to a kidney infection or even permanent kidney damage.

Self-Exams It is important for females to monitor their own bodies for signs of possible medical problems. Symptoms of vaginitis or cystitis, sores on the genitals, or any unusual pain in the abdomen require a medical exam. A female should also consult a doctor if she notices heavier bleeding than normal during menstruation, if her periods stop completely, or if she notices bleeding at times in between her regular periods.

Teen girls and women should also examine their breasts on a monthly basis for signs of breast cancer, one of the most common forms of cancer in females. Breast cancer is rare in teens, but it becomes more common as women age. The teen years are a good time to establish a lifetime habit of regular breast self-exams. If breast cancer is found early, the disease can be treated effectively and often cured.

Figure 12 outlines the procedure for the breast self-exam. The best time to do a breast self-exam is the week after a menstrual period, when the breasts are least swollen. For females who have not yet started menstruating, who have irregular periods, or who have reached menopause, the exam should be done on the same day each month. If you forget a month, don't worry. Resume the regular exams once you remember.

FIGURE 12 Females should follow this procedure to perform the breast self-exam.
Interpreting Diagrams Describe the motion that is recommended for ensuring that the entire breast area is checked.

Breast Self-Exam

1 Check your breasts while lying down.

▶ Lie down and place your right arm behind your head. Use the finger pads of the three middle fingers on your left hand to feel for lumps in the right breast.

▶ Use overlapping, dime-sized circular motions of the finger pads and three different levels of pressure. Use light pressure to feel the tissue closest to the skin. Use medium pressure to feel a little deeper. Use firm pressure to feel the tissue closest to the chest and ribs.

▶ Feel the breast in an up-and-down pattern starting at an imaginary line drawn straight down your side from the underarm (see diagram). Move inward until you reach your sternum, the bone in the middle of your chest.

▶ Check the entire breast area, moving down until you can feel only ribs, and moving up to your collar bone.

▶ Continue lying down. Lower your right hand and place your left arm above your head. Repeat the exam on your left breast, using the finger pads of the right hand.

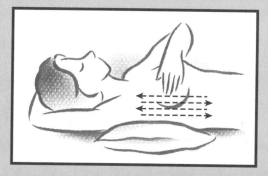

2 Look at your breasts while standing in front of a mirror.

While pressing your hands down firmly on your hips, look for any change in breast shape or appearance, such as dimpling of the skin, redness or swelling, or changes to the nipples.

3 Examine each underarm.

While standing or sitting, slightly raise your right arm and feel your underarm with your lefthand fingers. Repeat on your left side.

4 Report any abnormalities to your doctor immediately.

Many lumps are cysts or harmless tumors that are not cancerous, but only a doctor can make a diagnosis.

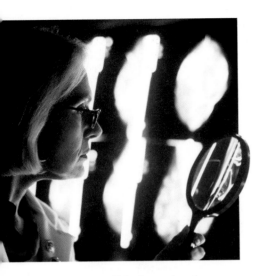

FIGURE 13 This doctor is using a magnifying glass to more closely examine a mammogram. A mammogram may detect cancers that are too small for a woman or her doctor to feel in a breast exam.

Medical Checkups A yearly checkup of the reproductive system is recommended for all females who have reached puberty. During the exam, the doctor will examine the breasts and genitals. The doctor is also likely to perform a pelvic exam if the female is over 18 or sexually active.

During the pelvic exam, the doctor inserts two gloved fingers into the vagina and places the other hand on the patient's abdomen. This way the doctor can feel the size and shape of the uterus and ovaries and check for any swelling, growths, or tenderness. The doctor may also perform a **Pap smear,** a test for cervical cancer. The doctor inserts an instrument called a speculum into the vagina, which holds the walls of the vagina apart. Next the doctor gently scrapes some cells from the cervix. The cells are sent to a laboratory and examined under a microscope for signs of cancer.

Starting at about age 40, women may get a **mammogram,** an X-ray of the breast that can help detect breast cancer. A woman with a family history of breast cancer or other risk factors may have her first mammogram at a younger age.

A doctor can also detect and treat other reproductive problems, including cancers of the ovary or uterus, and the following:

▶ **Ovarian cysts** Ovarian cysts are growths on the ovary. Large ones may be painful and need to be surgically removed.

▶ **Endometriosis** This is a condition in which tissue from the lining of the uterus—the endometrium—grows outside the uterus, in the pelvic cavity. This condition can be very painful and is usually treated with hormones or surgery.

▶ **Infertility** Causes of infertility in women include blocked fallopian tubes and problems with ovulation.

Section 2 Review

Key Ideas and Vocabulary

1. What are three main functions of the female reproductive system?
2. What is **ovulation**?
3. What event marks the end of one menstrual cycle and the beginning of another?
4. List five things that females should do to maintain reproductive health.

Critical Thinking

5. Calculating If a woman's ovaries release one egg per month for 30 years, how many eggs in total will she have released? **MATH**

Health at School

Medication Regulations Many girls suffer from menstrual cramps, sometimes during school hours. Ask your school nurse or an administrator what the policies are for taking pain medications on school grounds to treat menstrual cramps and other common aches and pains. Write a memo detailing your findings. **WRITING**

6. Applying Concepts How could more young women be convinced of the importance of regular breast self-exams? **WRITING**

Discovery EDUCATION **TEENS Talk**

Taking Charge of Your Health In what ways did the video motivate you to take charge of your health?

Reviewing Key Ideas

Section 1

1. Which of the following is *not* a structure in the male reproductive system?
   a. epididymis   b. seminal vesicle
   c. uterus   d. vas deferens

2. In males, straining to lift heavy objects may result in
   a. an inguinal hernia.
   b. an enlarged prostate.
   c. testicular cancer.
   d. infertility.

3. For which of the following should a male seek immediate medical attention?
   a. erections for no apparent reason
   b. testicular torsion
   c. nocturnal emission
   d. breast tenderness

4. What are the reproductive glands called in males?

5. What are two effects of testosterone?

6. Describe the roles played by hormones during sperm production.

7. Describe the route of sperm from the testes to the penis.

8. List three possible causes of infertility in men.

9. **Critical Thinking** Steroids abused by some athletes to build muscle contain chemicals similar to sex hormones. Why do you think steroid use can have a harmful effect on the reproductive system, especially in teens?

10. **Critical Thinking** Only one sperm is needed to fertilize an egg, yet millions of sperm are released during ejaculation. Why do you think this is?

Health and Community

Cancer Awareness Write a script for a public service announcement to raise awareness about prostate or breast cancer. Think about the age of the people you want to target with your message. Develop your message to best reach that audience. **WRITING**

Section 2

11. Which organ releases mature eggs?
    a. hymen   b. pituitary gland
    c. vagina   d. ovary

12. How long is the average menstrual cycle?
    a. 3 to 5 days   b. 14 days
    c. 28 days   d. 9 months

13. Explain how the functions of the uterus and cervix are related.

14. In which reproductive structure does fertilization usually take place?

15. Name two hormones that play a role in the menstrual cycle.

16. Which kind of cancer may be detected by a Pap smear?

17. **Critical Thinking** Your 13-year-old sister does not menstruate regularly. Should she be concerned? Explain.

Building Health Skills

18. **Accessing Information** Suppose that your younger brother is worried because he's been hearing a lot of myths about puberty from his classmates. How could you help him find accurate information?

19. **Advocacy** Suppose that a friend has confided in you that during a breast self-exam, she detected a lump. She is reluctant to see a doctor. Write an e-mail to your friend with advice. **WRITING**

20. **Communicating** What kinds of questions might a teenager want to ask the doctor during puberty? Make a list of possible questions for someone of your gender.

21. **Practicing Healthful Behaviors** What important health decisions can you make to keep your reproductive system healthy? Describe at least three decisions and explain what positive effect those decisions can have. **WRITING**

Responsible Relationships

Go Online
PHSchool.com

Discovery
EDUCATION™

TEENS Talk

CLASSROOM VIDEO #6

Choosing Abstinence

Preview Activity

What Do Your Choices Say About You?

Complete this activity before you watch the video.

1. Think about this quote.
   It is our choices that show what we truly are, far more than our abilities.
2. Then write a short paragraph describing what the quote means to you. **WRITING**
3. Pair up with another student to share and discuss your paragraphs.

Dating Relationships

Objectives

▶ **List** some things you can learn about a person by dating.

▶ **Describe** some strategies for dealing with dating concerns.

Vocabulary

• infatuation

Warm-Up

Quick Quiz Which of these do you value most in a romantic partner?

(1) Someone who is physically attractive

(2) Someone who is outgoing

(3) Someone who is intelligent

(4) Someone who is honest and reliable

(5) Someone who shares my values

WRITING Explain why you selected the answer that you did.

Physical Attraction and Dating

The teenage years are a time when most young people begin to experience feelings of physical attraction. Have you ever had a "crush" on a movie star, athlete, teacher, or other person you admire? Most teenagers have. Another name for these feelings of intense attraction to another person is **infatuation.** Although these feelings can sometimes be overwhelming, they are normal and healthy for teenagers. From these feelings, you develop the ability to form close attachments later in your adult life.

When you are attracted to someone, you want to spend time with that person. Some people use the term *dating* to describe the time you spend together. **By dating someone, you can learn about his or her interests, personality, abilities, and values.** You can also learn how the other person views the gender roles that he or she learned as a child. You may even discover what qualities you want in a future marriage partner.

Dating practices vary with individuals, families, and cultures. Some teens don't date at all during high school because they don't want to or because dating is not permitted in their culture. When teens do date, some stick to traditional practices. For example, females may wait for males to ask them out, or expect the males to pay for the date. Today, however, many dating arrangements are more informal than in the past.

Going Out as a Group   Dating often grows out of group activities that include both males and females. A group of teens may enjoy bowling on a Saturday afternoon, for example. Or they might go to a school sports event and meet for pizza afterward. There are advantages to doing things as a group. It gives you an opportunity to see how people behave when they are with others. In return, they get to know more about you.

Going Out as Couples   During group activities you may discover that you especially enjoy being with a certain friend. The person may be someone who shares your interests or has a similar sense of humor. You also may be physically attracted to this person. It is natural and healthy to feel physical attraction and to want to get to know the person better. This may lead to dating, either on your own or with other couples.

Steady Dating   After a few dates, a couple may decide not to date others and to see each other on a regular basis. Steady dating can be a form of security—partners are guaranteed a date whenever the need arises.

Steady dating has some drawbacks. You limit your chances of meeting other people you might like. You may feel pressured to make decisions about sexual intimacy before you are ready. If conflicts arise, it may be difficult to break off the relationship.

For some couples, steady dating leads to marriage. For couples that marry as teens, there are challenges beyond those faced by most married couples. These challenges include limited job skills, a lack of emotional maturity, loss of freedom, and loss of shared activities with friends.

FIGURE 1   If you go out as a group or as couples, you get to know many different people. You also get to observe how a person who you are attracted to interacts with others.

Connect to YOUR LIFE   Do you think steady dating during high school is a good idea? Why or why not?

MEDIA Wise

Gender Roles and Movies

People learn about gender roles by observing how other people behave. Family members, friends, and other adults may serve as roles models. People also receive messages about gender roles from movies. Use this checklist to evaluate how gender roles are shown in a movie.

Do the females tend to be less assertive than the males?	Yes No
Are the male roles more action-oriented than the female roles?	Yes No
Do the females share their feelings more easily than the males?	Yes No
When there is a problem to solve, is the problem solver usually male?	Yes No
Do the men tend to work outside the home and the women inside the home?	Yes No

Two or more "Yes" answers indicate a movie that supports traditional gender roles.

Activity Use the checklist to evaluate gender roles in two movies. Then write a paragraph about what you observed. How do you think these movies affect people's opinions about gender roles? **WRITING**

Dating Concerns

Dating can be a stressful experience, even for adults. People often feel both excitement and anxiety before and during a date. They want to make a good impression. They worry about doing or saying the wrong thing. Teens often have an added concern—their family's expectations. **There are ways to make the dating experience less stressful. You can be yourself, communicate honestly, learn to handle rejection, and address your family's concerns.**

Be Yourself People often say that the best approach in social situations is to "be yourself." This is good advice because it takes energy to put on an act, and it is hard to keep up an act over time. Being yourself does not mean doing whatever you want without any concern for others. It does mean, for example, that if you are shy, you do not have to try to be the center of attention. Or if you are cautious, you do not have to be daring in order to impress others.

If feelings of shyness or insecurity keep you from dating, focus on ways you can meet new people and build your confidence. Join a club, volunteer to help plan a school event, or sign up for a school trip.

Connect to YOUR LIFE What concerns do you have about dating?

Communicate Honestly   Even the most confident teens can feel awkward or self-conscious on occasion. If both people know what to expect on a date, the experience is likely to be less awkward. Use the questions in Figure 2 to discuss your plans with your date.

If you are honest, you can avoid many misunderstandings. For example, suppose someone asks you to go hiking, which you don't normally do. Make sure the person knows that you haven't been hiking before and are concerned about being able to keep up. With this information, the person could plan a shorter or less challenging hike.

If a date doesn't work out as planned, don't overreact. Your date will be impressed if you show that you can cope with unexpected events.

Learn to Handle Rejection   When you ask someone out, the person may say no. Or after a first date, a person may not agree to a second. Here are some tips for handling rejection.

▶ Don't let fear of rejection keep you from asking someone out.

▶ Don't let a *no* lead to self-doubt. The person may not be ready for a relationship or may not share your interests.

▶ Just because one person says *no* that doesn't mean that other people will not want to go out with you.

Address Your Family's Concerns   Dating is often an area of conflict between teens and adults. Adults may fear that dating will lead to risky behaviors, such as drug use, sexual activity, and reckless driving. It helps if you can talk calmly with your family about their concerns. It also helps if you share the answers to the questions in Figure 2 with them.

Parents and guardians never stop worrying about their children. But their fears may decrease if you follow the rules, tell the truth about what you are doing, and let your family meet the people you date.

Tips for Dating

Before you go out, ask:
- Where are we going?
- How will we get there?
- Is anyone else going?
- What will it cost and who will pay?
- When will we be back?
- How can I be reached in an emergency?

FIGURE 2   You improve your chances of having a successful dating experience if you ask the right questions in advance.

Section 1 Review

Key Ideas and Vocabulary

1. What does the term **infatuation** mean?

2. List four things people can learn by dating.

3. What can you do to make the dating experience less stressful?

4. Why do adults worry when teens begin to date?

Critical Thinking

5. Applying Concepts Suppose someone you really like invites you to go rock climbing. The person doesn't know that you have a fear of heights. How should you handle this situation?

Health at School

Honest Communication With three of your classmates, write a short skit that shows the importance of honest communication. Pick a situation where failing to ask questions, or telling a lie when answering a question, causes a misunderstanding. **WRITING**

6. Comparing and Contrasting What are some differences between infatuation and dating?

7. Predicting Blanca's mother finds out that Blanca lied about where she went and who she was with on Saturday night. How might this lie affect Blanca's relationship with her mother?

Choosing Abstinence

Objectives

▶ **Identify** some risks of sexual intimacy.

▶ **Explain** why emotional intimacy is important in close relationships.

▶ **List** some skills that can help you choose abstinence.

Vocabulary

• emotional intimacy
• abstinence

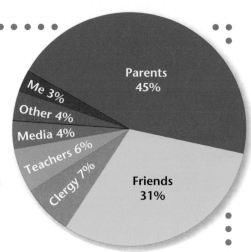

Warm-Up

Health Stats Who has the most influence on a teen's decisions about sex? The graph shows how some teens responded to this question.

WRITING Which influences do you think would help teens to make healthy decisions about sex? Explain.

Parents 45%
Me 3%
Other 4%
Media 4%
Teachers 6%
Clergy 7%
Friends 31%

Risks of Sexual Intimacy

As teenagers become aware of their sexuality, some tough questions arise: How can I show affection without things going too far? Are my partner and I emotionally ready for a sexual relationship? There are no easy answers for such questions. It is important, however, to think about these questions before you have to make decisions that can affect the rest of your life.

As you think about sexual intimacy, there are some important issues for you to consider. **Sexual intimacy is not risk free. The risks include the effect on your emotional health, the effect on your relationship, the risk of pregnancy, and the risk of sexually transmitted infections.**

Effect on Your Emotional Health Decisions about sexual intimacy should be based on the values that you hold. Your family, friends, religion, culture, experiences, and the media help shape your values. Often the messages you receive from different sources will be contradictory. This makes it more difficult to sort out how you truly feel.

A decision to become sexually involved may go against a person's values. If the person makes the decision anyway, the person may feel guilty or ashamed. The person may feel that he or she has let down parents, friends, and others as well as himself or herself. The result of making snap decisions about sex is often a loss of self-respect. Using sex to prove something to oneself and others can also lower self-esteem.

Effect on Your Relationship   A decision to become sexually intimate alters the way couples spend their time together. It also changes the way a couple relates to friends. Sexual intimacy can affect each person's expectations. One person may expect to have sex whenever the couple is together, while the other person may not. One person may become more possessive and put more demands on the other's time. One person may decide to end the relationship.

Often couples are not prepared for the complications that sexual intimacy adds to their relationship. Most couples find that these changes to their relationship are permanent. Although they may try, it is almost impossible to go back to the way things were before they had sex.

Risk of Pregnancy   A teenage pregnancy can pose serious health problems for the baby and the mother. Babies born to young mothers are often smaller and less healthy than those born to older women. Teenage mothers are more likely to have health problems during pregnancy than women in their twenties. This is because pregnant teenagers do not always eat well or get adequate medical care during pregnancy, especially in the early months.

Besides health problems, what effect does a baby have on a teenage couple? Parents are legally responsible to care for their children. Teenage parents often report feeling overwhelmed and trapped. Many teenage mothers drop out of school. Some fathers don't help support or care for the child; others drop out of school and work at low-paying jobs.

Young people are aware of the problems teenage parents face, but they often don't think that pregnancy can happen to them. Few teens want to become pregnant. But one in six teenage girls who engage in sexual intercourse becomes pregnant. Sexual intimacy is a high-risk behavior for anyone who isn't ready to accept the responsibility of children.

Connect to YOUR LIFE   What effect might a pregnancy have on a teenage couple's relationship?

FIGURE 3   After caring for a baby, a teenage mother may not have enough energy left for school. **Predicting** How could dropping out of school affect the mother? How could it affect the baby?

About 25% of teen mothers have a second baby before age 20.

Risk of Sexually Transmitted Infections Some infections can be passed, or transmitted, from one person to another during sexual activity. These are called sexually transmitted infections, or STIs. If left untreated, many STIs cause serious health problems. For example, some STIs can cause infertility, or the inability to have children. Others shorten a person's life or require medical treatment throughout a person's life.

Emotional Intimacy

Contrary to what you may think, every teen is not sexually experienced. Millions of young people today choose to postpone sexual activity. On a television show, a young man spoke of his relationship with his girlfriend. "We're not ready for sex, but we share lots of other intimate experiences."

How can two people be intimate without being sexually involved? They can trust each other with personal feelings or dreams that they haven't told anyone else. They can exchange "inside" jokes. They can do kind things for each other and be best friends.

Emotional intimacy refers to the openness, sharing, affection, and trust that can develop in a close relationship. Two things can help a couple develop emotional intimacy. They must be honest with one another. They must be accepting and supportive of each other. **A couple can have a close relationship without being sexually intimate. But it is hard for them to keep a relationship close if there is no emotional intimacy.**

Abstinence Skills

Sergio and Selena met in class and became good friends. Soon, they started to date. As they spent more time together, they began to express their feelings of affection by hugging, kissing, and holding hands. Over time, the pressure to become more physically intimate grew stronger. But Sergio and Selena felt that abstinence was the best choice at this point in their lives.

Abstinence is the act of refraining from, or not having, sex. There are skills you can learn to help you choose abstinence when you are faced with the pressure to become more physically intimate. **These abstinence skills include setting clear limits, communicating your limits, avoiding high-pressure situations, and asserting yourself.**

FIGURE 4 Trust and affection are two signs of strong emotional bonds. These bonds form when couples are honest and supportive of one another.

FIGURE 5 It is important to discuss your limits on sexual intimacy as early as possible in a relationship. **Evaluating** Which communication skills are most important when you want to clearly state your limits?

Set Clear Limits It is natural to feel sexual attraction to someone you are dating. It is also natural to be unsure of how to handle these feelings. Most teenagers try to think ahead and set limits for expressing their sexual feelings. If you set limits before a situation arises, it will be easier to stick to the standards you set. Take some time now to set limits that you feel comfortable with. It is important to know your limits before you go out so you can avoid having to make a hasty decision.

To help yourself set limits, be sure to consider the important values that you hold and the possible consequences of your actions. It is essential that you make decisions with which you feel comfortable. Do not allow the expectations of friends, the media, and others to influence you to make decisions that may not be right for you.

Communicate Your Limits Once you have decided on your limits, it is important to communicate your feelings to your partner. Of course, it is best to discuss things as early as possible in a relationship. Do not wait until a situation arises in which your partner's expectations may be different from yours. It may be difficult to have an open, constructive discussion if you wait until that point to talk.

Try to talk honestly to your partner about your feelings and values. You may be surprised at how relieved your partner may be to hear how you feel. He or she may have been anxious about your expectations.

If you have been sexually involved, it doesn't mean that you have to continue to be sexually involved. You may decide that a relationship built around emotional intimacy makes more sense, and choose abstinence. If your partner tries to make you feel guilty, you may need to rethink your relationship. Do you really want to be with a person who does not respect your feelings or who does not value emotional intimacy?

For: Updates on abstinence
Visit: www.SciLinks.org/health
Web Code: ctn-2064

Are you comfortable talking with friends about your values? Why or why not?

FIGURE 6 One way for couples to avoid high-pressure situations is to go out as a group.

Avoid High-Pressure Situations   Sticking to the limits you set can be difficult. You can make it easier for yourself by avoiding certain situations. For example, if you are at an unsupervised party, you might feel pressured to have sex. But if you are in a public place, the temptation to engage in sexual activities is not as great. It is also important to avoid alcohol and other drugs, as they can blur your ability to think clearly.

Spend time with friends who share your values. You might want to include your date in family outings. Not only will you not be tempted to have sex, you will see how your date interacts with different people.

Assert Yourself   If you find yourself in a situation where you are not comfortable with the level of physical intimacy, don't feel guilty about saying no. State clearly and directly that you want to stop. You may want to offer a reason, such as "I'm just not ready," so that the other person won't feel hurt or rejected.

At times, however, simply saying no once may not be effective. You may need to be firm and say something like "No! I said I don't want to do that." You may need to repeat yourself a few times before your partner realizes that you are serious. If necessary, get up and walk away.

One person may try to pressure another by saying that, at some levels of intimacy, it is impossible to stop without causing physical harm. This isn't true. The person might also say things like "If you loved me, you would do it," or "Everybody does it." Remember that you will respect yourself more for sticking to your limits than for giving in to pressure.

If your partner does not respect the limits you set, the relationship may not be worth continuing. Try to meet people who understand the importance of dealing responsibly with sexual feelings. Look for people who value emotional intimacy.

Section 2 Review

Key Ideas and Vocabulary

1. What are four possible risks of sexual intimacy?

2. Define **emotional intimacy.**

3. How can emotional intimacy help a relationship to grow?

4. What is **abstinence?** What skills can help you to choose abstinence?

Critical Thinking

5. **Making Judgments** Review the risks of sexual intimacy. Which risk would be most likely to keep you from being sexually intimate? Give a reason for your choice.

Health at Home

Comparing Viewpoints Work with a parent or another trusted adult. Select two letters about teenage sexual choices from an advice column in a newspaper. Separately, the two of you should write responses to the letters. Then compare your responses to each other's and to the actual advice offered in the newspaper. **WRITING**

6. **Applying Concepts** How could a person who doesn't want to be sexually involved respond to each of these "pressure" lines?

a. "If you loved me, you would have sex with me."

b. "Everyone else is having sex. What's wrong with you?"

c. "You know you want to. Everyone wants to."

Unhealthy Relationships

Objectives
- ▶ **Describe** the cycle of violence.
- ▶ **Identify** reasons why a person should report a rape.
- ▶ **Explain** the effect of sexual abuse on a victim.
- ▶ **Describe** an effective way to reduce sexual harassment at school.

Vocabulary
- dating violence
- physical abuse
- emotional abuse
- sexual abuse
- rape
- date rape
- statutory rape
- incest
- pedophilia
- sexual harassment

Warm-Up

Myth A person who is raped is usually attacked by a stranger.

Fact Most victims of rape know their attackers.

WRITING What precautions could someone take to reduce the risk of being raped by a friend or acquaintance?

Violence in Dating Relationships

Unfortunately, some teen relationships turn violent. One partner may slap the other when he or she is angry. Or make fun of the other's looks or abilities. Or constantly check up to find out what the person is doing. These are examples of dating violence. **Dating violence** is a pattern of physical, emotional, or sexual abuse that occurs in a dating relationship.

▶ **Physical Abuse** Intentionally causing physical harm to another person is called **physical abuse.** A person who has frequent bruises may say "I tripped" or "I walked into a door." A more likely explanation is that he or she is a victim of physical abuse.

▶ **Emotional Abuse** "You never do anything right." "Without me, you're nothing." A person who constantly hears negative statements like these is likely to suffer from emotional abuse. **Emotional abuse** is the nonphysical mistreatment of a person. Emotional abuse does not leave visible scars. But it does leave victims feeling inadequate, helpless, or worthless. They may also feel anxious or depressed.

▶ **Sexual Abuse** When one person forces another to engage in any unwanted sexual behavior, the person is committing **sexual abuse.** The abuser may use physical force to get the victim to cooperate. He or she may also use threats or bribes.

Cycle of Violence

Violent Episode
• Uses force.
• May use a weapon.
• Causes serious injury.
• May destroy possessions.

Tension-Building
• Picks fights.
• Acts jealous and possessive.
• Criticizes or threatens.
• Has unpredictable mood swings.
• Isolates victim from others.

Calm
• Asks for forgiveness.
• Makes promises.
• Buys presents.
• Is affectionate.
• Denies the abuse happened.

FIGURE 7 The cycle of violence is a repeated pattern of tension-building, violent episodes, and calm. Over time, the cycle may shorten. The tension-building and calm stages may disappear, leaving only a series of violent episodes. **Predicting** What control does the victim have over the cycle of violence?

The Cycle of Violence   Often abuse occurs as part of the three-stage cycle in Figure 7. **The cycle of violence consists of a tension-building stage, a violent episode, and a calm or "honeymoon" stage.** During the tension-building stage, the victim may try to please the abuser or reason with the abuser in order to prevent violence. Sometimes victims describe this stage as "walking on eggshells." The tension is broken by a violent episode.

During the calm stage, the abuser may apologize and promise to never abuse the victim again. The abuser may also blame the victim for the abuse. The calm is followed by another tension-building stage.

The Need for Control   Why would a person abuse someone that he or she claims to care about? Experts agree that the major reason people abuse others is the need for control. Odd as it may seem, abusers tend to see themselves as victims. They think that they have the right to control an intimate relationship. Being able to control another person makes them feel powerful.

Warning Signs of Abuse   A good way to avoid the cycle of violence is to recognize the warning signs that can lead to abuse.

▶ Your date is jealous when you talk to others.

▶ Your date makes all the decisions and tries to control what you do.

▶ Your date has a history of bad relationships.

▶ You feel isolated from your friends and family.

▶ You feel less self-confident when you are with your date.

▶ You change how you behave to avoid an argument.

Ending the Abuse   Why would a teen remain in an abusive relationship or hide the abuse from others? Some teens may view a possessive or jealous partner as romantic. Or they may think the behavior is normal because friends are in similar relationships. Females may think that males are supposed to act in a controlling manner or that physical aggression is a sign of masculinity. Males may be ashamed to admit that they are being abused for fear of being seen as weak. Sadly, some teens may think that they deserve to be abused. Others may fear being alone.

The first step to ending an abusive relationship is to admit that the abuse exists. The second step is to realize that you are not to blame for the abuse and that you cannot change how your abuser behaves. Seek the support of friends and family. Call an abuse hotline if you want anonymous advice. Talk to a counselor, teacher, doctor, or social worker, but be aware that these adults are legally required to report abuse.

Rape

When one person forces another to have sex, the act is called **rape.** Although rape is a problem for both females and males, the majority of victims are female.

Date Rape   Most women who are raped know the person who raped them. The person may have been an acquaintance, a casual date, or a steady date. Rape that occurs during a date is often called **date rape.**

The rapist may have used a "date rape drug." These fast-acting drugs are hard to detect in food or a drink because they are colorless, tasteless, and odorless. Later, the victim will feel "hung over" and be unable to recall the rape. Friends will say that the victim acted drunk. It is important to do what you can to decrease your chances of being raped by a date or acquaintance. Figure 8 lists some tips for dating safely.

Statutory Rape   Date rape is a crime. So is having sex with someone the state considers too young to give his or her consent. Having sex with someone who is under the age of consent is called **statutory rape.** The age of consent varies among states, from age 14 to age 18. A state is more likely to charge a person with rape when the age difference is greater than three years.

Reporting Rape   Some people don't report rapes, especially date rapes. They may be ashamed, feel responsible, or think they won't be believed. **But reporting a rape is important so the victim can receive medical attention and counseling. Also, law enforcement can collect evidence needed to prosecute the rapist and prevent future rapes.** A person who is raped should contact the police or a rape crisis center. Either group can arrange for the person to see a doctor or nurse. A counselor can discuss the risks of STIs and offer females a drug to prevent a possible pregnancy.

Tips for Dating Safely

- Go out as a group.
- Let someone know where you are going.
- Avoid alcohol or other drugs.
- Have money to get home.
- In an emergency, call 911.

FIGURE 8   These tips can help decrease the chances of date rape.

Figure 9 This poster is advocating against the sexual abuse of children. **Predicting** Who do you think is the intended audience for this poster?

Sexual Abuse of Children

Accurate data on how many children and adolescents are victims of sexual abuse by adults are hard to find. Many cases are not reported. Typically, the adult is someone the victim knows well. The adult may be a parent, stepparent, older sibling, other relative, or a family friend.

Incest Sex between people who are too closely related to marry legally is called **incest.** Incest is a crime in all states, but the definition varies. All states consider sex between family members who are biologically related to be incest. Some states also define incest to include relationships based on adoption or remarriage. Whatever the legal definition, sexual behavior that feels wrong *is* wrong. The victim of the abuse should seek help.

Pedophilia Sometimes children are abused by a person with a mental disorder called pedophilia. People with **pedophilia** (ped uh FIL ee uh) have a sexual attraction to children. These people are known as pedophiles, or child molesters. They are almost always male. Some abuse family members. Others abuse children who are not related to them.

Ending the Abuse Even a single instance of sexual abuse can have a devastating effect. The victim feels guilty and ashamed. **In the victim's mind, he or she assumes all the responsibility or blame for the event.** It becomes difficult for the victim to trust others and develop caring relationships. Victims often experience symptoms of post-traumatic stress disorder, such as flashbacks and nightmares.

Victims of sexual abuse should talk with a trusted adult or call the Child Abuse Hotline. Deciding to seek help may be difficult. Victims risk angering, hurting, or betraying the abuser. If the abuser is a family member, sometimes other relatives don't want to believe what is going on and may accuse the victim of lying. The abuser may threaten the child to keep the child from telling. But it is more dangerous to believe the abuser's threats than to report the abuse. Remember, no one has the right to abuse you.

 What would you do if you knew a friend was being abused?

Sexual Harassment

Mariah's friend, Eduardo, told her that there were some explicit sexual comments about her in the boy's bathroom. She didn't pay much attention until a student she didn't know asked her for a sexual favor. What Maria experienced was sexual harassment.

Sexual harassment is any uninvited and unwelcome sexual remark or sexual advance. Making comments about a person's body parts is an example. So is unwanted touching or spreading rumors about someone's sexual behavior. Telling crude jokes in study hall is also an example. The jokes may make some students uncomfortable.

Sadly, sometimes the person doing the harassing is an adult. The difference in power between the adult and the student makes the behavior even less acceptable. **If school administrators, teachers, and students work together, they can stop sexual harassment.**

Go Online
HEALTH LINKS

For: Updates on dating responsibly
Visit: www.SciLinks.org/health
Web Code: ctn-2063

What Schools Must Do   Sexual harassment in schools is illegal. The administration at a school is required by law to respond quickly and forcefully when students complain about sexual harassment. If the school doesn't act, and the harassment continues, the victim has grounds to sue the harasser and the school.

What You Can Do   Here are ways you can stop sexual harassment.

▶ Speak up assertively when you feel disrespected.

▶ Use your refusal skills to reject unwanted sexual advances.

▶ Avoid having to be alone with someone you don't trust.

▶ Report behavior that you think is sexual harassment to an adult.

Section 3 Review

Key Ideas and Vocabulary

1. What is **dating violence?**
2. Describe the cycle of violence that can occur in a relationship.
3. Why should a person report a rape?
4. How does sexual abuse affect a victim?
5. What is **sexual harassment?** What is an effective way to stop sexual harassment at school?

Critical Thinking

6. **Comparing and Contrasting** What do physical abuse and emotional abuse have in common?
7. **Applying Concepts** Why would an abuser want to isolate a victim from family and friends?

Health and Community

Help Combat Dating Violence Find out about volunteer organizations in your community that deal with dating violence. For example, you could baby-sit for children at a local women's shelter. Or invite a police officer to talk about dating violence at a school assembly. Then write a paragraph summarizing what you learned. **WRITING**

8. **Evaluating** When Tamara's friends complain about how Dillon treats Tamara, she usually makes excuses for him. She says that he is under a lot of pressure and that her behavior often angers him. What advice would you give Tamara about her relationship with Dillon? **WRITING**

Sexual Issues in Society

Objectives

▶ **List** three rules to follow to use the Internet safely.

▶ **Describe** two industries that profit from sexual exploitation.

Vocabulary

• prostitution
• pornography

Warm-Up

Dear Advice Line,

I really like this guy I met in a chat room. He and I share so many interests. Lately he has been asking me to come and meet him in person. I have enough money for the bus trip from my town to his.

WRITING   What advice would you give this person?

Internet Safety

You probably know some basic rules for avoiding abuse by a stranger. When you are home alone, keep the doors locked and don't open the door for a stranger. Never let a caller know you are home alone. Avoid dark or deserted places. Keep your doors locked when driving and park in a well-lit place. Do not hitchhike or pick up a hitchhiker.

There is a similar list of rules you should know to protect yourself when you use the Internet. **Keep your identity private, be wary of people you meet online, and don't respond to inappropriate messages.** By following these rules, you can reduce the risks of using the Internet while enjoying the benefits.

Keep Your Identity Private   A Web site may ask you for information about yourself before letting you access the site. It may ask for your mailing address, phone number, age, and gender. You may be offered a free gift or a chance to enter a contest. Be cautious. The site may not be what it appears to be. The person who set up the site may be looking for someone to harm. The more personal the questions, the more cautious you should be. Be even more cautious if the site has sexual content.

Some teens have their own Web sites. Most teens post material on other people's Web sites. When you post something on the Web, never include your home address, telephone number, or a photograph. Also remember that any information you send to one person in an e-mail, including photographs, can easily be forwarded to many people.

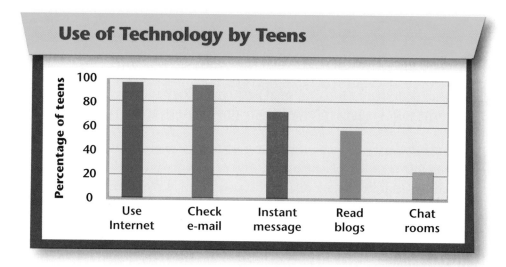

Use of Technology by Teens

FIGURE 10 Teens were surveyed about which technologies they used at least once a week. The results show why it is important for teens to know how to use the Internet safely. **Calculating** Based on the graph, how many students in a class of 30 students are likely to read blogs? **MATH**

Be Wary of People You Meet Online Chatting online with others who share your interests can be fun. You might even learn something. But there are risks. To protect yourself, remember not to share information that could be used to identify you. Avoid saying things you would not say if you were face to face with a group of people. Leave a chat room if people begin to talk about a topic that makes you feel uncomfortable.

Over time you may start to think of people you chat with regularly as friends. However, you don't know who these "friends" really are. Online, it is easy for a person to pretend to be a teen when he or she is really an adult. The person may also pretend to share your interests to attract your attention in hopes of taking advantage of you.

Ideally, you should never agree to meet with someone you chat with online. If you do decide to arrange a meeting, follow these rules. Someone who is telling the truth will understand your concerns.

▶ Always discuss your plans with a parent or guardian.

▶ Never go to a meeting by yourself.

▶ Arrange to meet in a public place that you are familiar with.

Don't Respond to Inappropriate Messages People who use the Internet often receive e-mails from people they do not know. Most are messages from people who are trying to sell a product or service. If you respond to these e-mails, the amount of unwanted e-mails, or "spam," that you receive is likely to multiply.

Sometimes people use e-mails, instant messaging, or chat rooms to threaten, or harass, other people. This behavior is called cyber bullying. If you get such a message, don't respond. If you continue to receive similar messages, show them to a parent or other trusted adult. Your Internet provider may be able to identify the source. Report any material that seems illegal to law enforcement. Examples include threats to your safety, threats against others, and sexually explicit images of children.

Connect to YOUR LIFE What are two specific actions you could take to increase your Internet safety?

Prostitution and Pornography

Some people are in the business of selling sex. Teens who get involved in such activities may do so because they need the money to survive. Or another person may force them to participate. **Two industries that make a profit from sexual exploitation are prostitution and pornography.**

Prostitution   When one person pays to have sex with another person, the activity is called **prostitution.** The person accepting the money, the prostitute, can be female or male. Prostitution is illegal in most states. Police usually arrest the prostitute, not the customer. Teens who run away from home may turn to prostitution to earn money for food or drugs. Surveys of teen prostitutes show that around forty percent of the girls and thirty percent of the boys were victims of sexual abuse at home.

A pimp is a person who finds clients for prostitutes. The pimp keeps most of the money the prostitute earns. Pimps target teenage runaways by pretending to be their friend. Frequently, the pimp uses drugs and physical violence to control a prostitute.

Pornography   Images and words that are designed to excite sexual arousal are called **pornography.** Pornography is difficult to define. But people tend to say that they know it when they see it. Everyone agrees that the use of children in pornography is exploitation. Making and distributing child pornography is also illegal.

Runaways may agree to make pornography because they are desperate for money. Other teens are lured by false promises of a modeling or acting career. Be suspicious of strangers who offer to take photographs of you for free. Also, don't let a friend talk you into posing for nude photographs or making a sexually explicit video. Think about what could happen to those images later on. They might end up on a Web site.

One-third of teens on the street are lured into prostitution within 48 hours.

FIGURE 11 Runaways are easy targets for people involved in pornography and prostitution.

Section 4 Review

Key Ideas and Vocabulary

1. What are three things you can do to protect yourself when you use the Internet?

2. Name two industries that make a profit from sexual exploitation.

3. Define **prostitution**.

4. What is **pornography**?

Critical Thinking

5. Relating Cause and Effect How could abuse within a family contribute to the problem of runaways?

Health at Home

Comparing Viewpoints Work with a parent or another trusted adult. Look at some profiles that teens have posted on a social networking Web site. Discuss your opinions of the profiles. Then write a paragraph summarizing the discussion, noting areas of agreement and areas of disagreement. **WRITING**

6. Applying Concepts Someone calls you at home and asks you to take a phone survey. Which rules about Internet safety would apply in this situation? Explain your answer.

Discovery EDUCATION **TEENS Talk**

Choosing Abstinence Describe three things you learned from the video about the benefits of choosing abstinence.

Reviewing Key Ideas

Section 1

1. An infatuation is characterized by
   a. intense physical attraction.
   b. honest communication.
   c. shared interests and values.
   d. mutual trust and acceptance.

2. What are some benefits of steady dating? What are some drawbacks?

3. What are three things you can do to help address your family's concerns about dating?

4. **Critical Thinking** Three weeks in a row you invite someone you like to go to the movies. Each time the person says "I would like to go, but I have other plans." Should you try again? Why or why not?

Section 2

5. The act of refraining from sex is called
   a. sexual intimacy.
   b. emotional intimacy.
   c. abstinence.
   d. sexual involvement.

6. In what ways does having a baby change the lives of teenage parents?

7. Describe two things a couple could do to increase their emotional intimacy.

8. Explain why it is important to think about your limits before you are faced with a decision about sexual intimacy.

9. **Critical Thinking** Jada's communication style is passive. How could this style lead to misunderstandings about sexual intimacy?

Health and Community

Community Guide for Teens Design a guide for teens who are new to your community. Describe things they can do to meet people. Include all the necessary details about the activities, such as times, dress codes, and costs. You may want to include a map with locations marked. **WRITING**

Section 3

10. The nonphysical mistreatment of a person is
    a. physical abuse.
    b. sexual abuse.
    c. emotional abuse.
    d. statutory rape.

11. List at least four reasons why a teen might remain in an abusive relationship.

12. What should a student do when faced with sexual harassment at school?

13. **Critical Thinking** Why is it as important to address emotional abuse as it is to deal with physical abuse?

14. **Critical Thinking** Why do you think that a child who is abused by an adult might feel responsible for the abuse?

Section 4

15. Why is it important to protect your identity when you use the Internet?

16. What should you do if you receive e-mails that contain threats?

17. **Critical Thinking** Besides being arrested, what risks do prostitutes face?

18. **Critical Thinking** What could a person who wants to run away from home do instead?

 ## Building Health Skills

19. **Making Decisions** Develop a list of rules to follow in a dating relationship. Make sure your rules emphasize respect for yourself and others.

20. **Setting Goals** Choose one of the abstinence skills you studied in Section 2. Make an action plan to apply this skill to situations other than choosing abstinence. For example, you could set clear limits not to be interrupted when you are doing your homework. Monitor your progress and adjust your action plan, if necessary. **WRITING**

21. **Advocacy** A friend who wants to be a model has been posing for suggestive photographs. What advice would you give your friend?

Planning
for the Future

Go Online
PHSchool.com

Discovery EDUCATION

TEENS Talk

CLASSROOM VIDEO #19

Teen Pregnancy

Preview Activity

How Would Your Plans Change?

Complete this activity before you watch the video.

1. Make a list of your plans for the weekend. Make a second list of your plans for after graduation.
2. Now suppose that you were a teen parent. Describe all the ways you think your weekend plans and your long-term plans would need to change. **WRITING**

Marriage and Family Decisions

Objectives

▶ **List** three keys to a successful marriage.

▶ **Identify** the lifelong responsibilities of parenthood.

Vocabulary

• compatibility
• commitment
• compromise

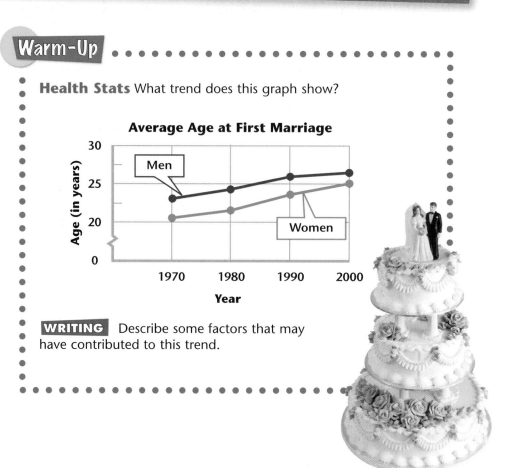

Warm-Up

Health Stats What trend does this graph show?

Average Age at First Marriage

WRITING Describe some factors that may have contributed to this trend.

Marriage

During adolescence, many teens start to think about what it would be like to be in a committed, long-term relationship such as marriage. Some teens look forward to making such a commitment. Others are reluctant. Some feel that they may never be ready to take such a step.

Approximately ninety percent of all Americans marry at some time during their lives. Therefore, it is highly likely that you will marry someday. If you do choose to marry, it will probably be one of the most important decisions you will make. It will affect you, your spouse, your family, your friends, and possibly future generations. Understanding the challenges of marriage can help you to know when you are ready to take such a step.

Connect to YOUR LIFE What do you think is the most important part of a successful marriage?

FIGURE 1 Successful marriages require the couple to make many adjustments, such as becoming members of different families.

Why People Marry People marry for a variety of reasons. Some people marry because they desire another person's love and companionship. Others marry for financial, social, or cultural reasons.

You need to know yourself fairly well before you select a marriage partner. You need to know what your goals are and how you are going to achieve them. You need to know what is important to you. When it comes time to marry, people usually select marriage partners who have similar interests, values, level of education, and social background to themselves. People who are quite different from each other can also have successful marriages, but they may have to work harder to overcome their differences.

Successful Marriages You probably feel, as most people do, that successful marriages are based on love. But what is love? Often young people mistake sexual attraction or short-lived crushes for love. Real love is part of a long-lasting relationship in which people really know, like, and accept each other. People who are truly in love appreciate the things they like about each other and accept the things they dislike. When you love someone, his or her well-being becomes as important to you as your own.

Although love is a basic element in a successful marriage, it is not the only one. **Love, compatibility, and commitment are key factors in a successful marriage. Compatibility** is the ability to live together in harmony. **Commitment** is the strong determination by the couple to make their marriage a fulfilling lifelong relationship.

There are several other important factors that contribute to most successful marriages.

▶ **Ability to Compromise** Even the most compatible couples will disagree occasionally. During a **compromise,** each partner gives up something to reach an agreement.

▶ **Communication** Partners should be able to share their thoughts and feelings. Each should trust the other to listen and accept what is being said without making judgments.

▶ **Sexual Intimacy** Sexual intimacy in marriage is an expression of mutual physical attraction, emotional intimacy, and love.

Stresses in Marriage   Throughout marriage, a couple must be willing to make adjustments to meet each other's needs. The changes in attitudes and expectations that these adjustments require can produce stress.

One difficult adjustment in marriage can be determining the responsibilities that each spouse will have. Some couples decide early in their marriage how each person will contribute financially and who will do certain household tasks. By compromising and accepting tasks that fit their abilities and schedules, a couple usually can develop a comfortable give-and-take relationship. When changes occur, such as the birth of a child, the couple may need to redefine their responsibilities.

Marriages can become strained when unexpected problems arise. One spouse may lose his or her job. A family member may become seriously ill. Effective communication can help a couple get through a crisis. Sometimes a couple may need to seek financial or counseling services. Turning to family or friends for emotional support is another way to get through hard times.

Teen Marriage   When teenagers marry, they often face additional challenges compared with those who marry later. The strains of adjusting to a new relationship, earning a living, and completing an education can feel overwhelming. Many married teenagers drop out of school. Without a high-school diploma, it can be difficult to find a good job. The couple may end up living with relatives. Such an arrangement can limit a couple's opportunities to make decisions and to develop as a couple.

Another difficulty for married teenagers involves changes in their friendships. Unmarried friends may not have the same interests and goals as a married couple, especially if the couple has a baby. A married couple may be concerned about stretching a small income, while single friends may be more concerned about school or dating.

It is difficult to know when you are 17 or 18 just who you will be when you are 25 or 30. People change a great deal during their teens and early twenties. For this reason, most teenagers choose to wait before making a long-term commitment. They want to find out more about themselves and to have other experiences first.

FIGURE 2   Divorce rates are typically higher for couples who marry in their teens.
Reading Graphs What percentage of marriages in which the wife is under age 18 when she marries end in divorce within the first five years?

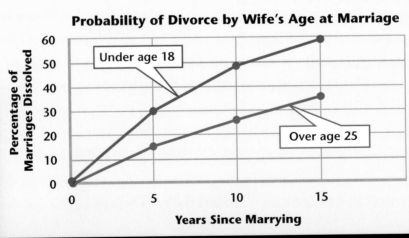

Probability of Divorce by Wife's Age at Marriage

Parenthood

For some people, adulthood is not only a time for marriage, but also a time to become parents. Parenthood has many joys and satisfactions, but it is also stressful and involves a lot of hard work. Along with the loving feelings, smiles, and cuddles, new parents face sleepless nights, worries about illnesses, and the loss of many freedoms they used to enjoy.

The responsibilities of parenthood go far beyond those of most occupations. **Parents need to be able to commit a lifetime of love, guidance, and attention to their children.** The relationship between parent and child is critical to the child's healthy development.

At least one part of making the decision to become parents is purely practical. A couple should review their budget to find out whether they can afford to provide food, clothing, and medical care for a child. They need to discuss who will care for the child if both spouses continue to work. They need to find out if their employers grant maternity or paternity leave, so that at least one of them can stay home with the baby for a few months and still return to the same job. They may also need to investigate the costs and availability of child care.

FIGURE 3 Before becoming parents, a couple should make sure they are ready to carry out the responsibilities of parenthood to the best of their ability.

Section 1 Review

Key Ideas and Vocabulary

1. What are three keys to a successful marriage?

2. Explain how **compatibility** contributes to a successful marriage.

3. What does **commitment** mean in the context of marriage?

4. Describe the lifelong responsibilities of parenthood.

Critical Thinking

5. Relating Cause and Effect What advice would you give to a friend who thinks that having a baby will help her relationship grow stronger?

Health and Community

An Interview With Adults Interview three adults—a young adult, a middle-aged adult, and an older adult. Ask them what advice they would offer to teenagers who are trying to set goals for the future. Compare the responses of the people you interviewed. What did you learn about planning for the future? **WRITING**

6. Applying Concepts Ryan and Linda have been arguing over how to spend some extra money. Ryan wants to buy a new car. Linda wants to buy new furniture. Suggest a way for Linda and Ryan to compromise.

Development Before Birth

Objectives

▶ **Summarize** the events that occur during the first week after fertilization.

▶ **Describe** the structures that protect and nourish the embryo and fetus.

Vocabulary

- zygote
- embryo
- blastocyst
- implantation
- amniotic sac
- placenta
- umbilical cord
- fetus

Warm-Up

Quick Quiz Which of the following statements made by a married couple do you think are good reasons for having a baby? Choose one or more.

① "It's now or never. We're almost 40."

② "We have lots of love to give a child."

③ "If we have one more, maybe it will be a girl."

④ "Our marriage will improve if we have a baby."

⑤ "With our new jobs, we've finally saved enough money to start a family."

WRITING In a paragraph, describe the factors you think a married couple should consider before they have children.

The Beginning of the Life Cycle

The birth of a baby is an incredible event. For parents, the nine months or so that precede their child's birth are filled with expectations. The years afterward are times of both hard work and wonder.

As a teenager, you may be curious about the physical processes of pregnancy. You may also think about the responsibilities and challenges that you may face one day as a parent. Understanding how human life begins and what pregnancy involves will help you to make responsible decisions now and in the future.

When a couple decides to start a family, they may try to conceive, or get pregnant. Recall from Chapter 2 that, in a fertile woman's body, about once a month an egg enters one of the fallopian tubes and begins its journey to the uterus. During sexual intercourse, sperm from the man are deposited into the vagina. Some of these sperm swim through the uterus to the fallopian tubes. If an egg is present in a fallopian tube, a sperm may fertilize it. This moment of fertilization is also called conception.

Sperm surrounding an egg ▼

❶ Fertilization In Figure 4, you can track the events that occur in the first week after fertilization. Of the hundreds of millions of sperm that enter the vagina during sexual intercourse, only a few hundred usually make it to the egg, and only one can fertilize it. Within seconds of fertilization, the surface of the egg changes so that no more sperm can enter the egg. **In the first week after fertilization, the fertilized egg undergoes many cell divisions and travels to the uterus.**

❷ The Zygote The united egg and sperm is called a **zygote** (ZY goht). Within 36 hours, while the zygote is still traveling through the fallopian tube, it begins to divide.

❸ Cell Division The original cell divides to make two cells. From the two-cell stage until about nine weeks after fertilization, the growing structure is called an **embryo** (EM bree oh). As the embryo travels toward the uterus, its cells continue to divide.

❹ The Blastocyst About five days after fertilization, the embryo reaches the uterus, where it floats for a few days. By this time, it is made up of about 50 to 100 cells. The structure, called a **blastocyst** (BLAS tuh sist), is no longer a solid mass of cells, but a sphere of cells with a hollow center.

❺ Implantation Once the blastocyst forms, it begins to attach itself to the wall of the uterus. The process of attachment is called **implantation.**

FIGURE 4 The fertilized egg travels to the uterus in the first week of pregnancy.
Interpreting Diagrams Through which structure does the embryo travel before reaching the uterus?

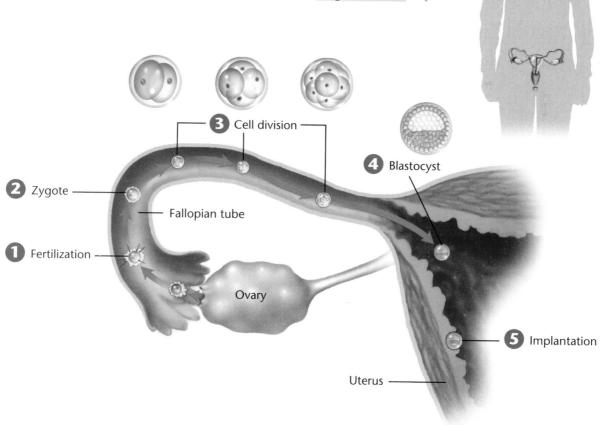

❸ Cell division

❷ Zygote

Fallopian tube

❶ Fertilization

Ovary

❹ Blastocyst

❺ Implantation

Uterus

FIGURE 5 The embryo is surrounded by several protective structures.

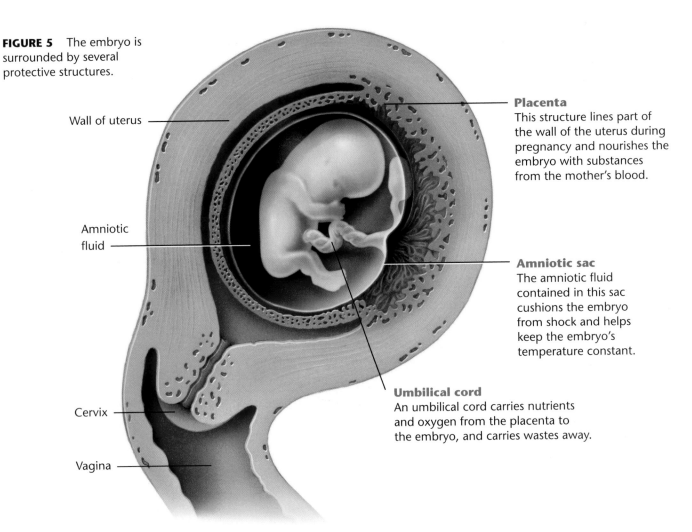

Wall of uterus

Amniotic fluid

Cervix

Vagina

Placenta
This structure lines part of the wall of the uterus during pregnancy and nourishes the embryo with substances from the mother's blood.

Amniotic sac
The amniotic fluid contained in this sac cushions the embryo from shock and helps keep the embryo's temperature constant.

Umbilical cord
An umbilical cord carries nutrients and oxygen from the placenta to the embryo, and carries wastes away.

Development in the Uterus

After implantation, development continues in the uterus. While the embryo grows, several other structures that you can see in Figure 5 also develop. **These structures—the amniotic sac, placenta, and umbilical cord—protect and nourish the developing embryo, and later the fetus.**

Amniotic Sac Soon after implantation, a fluid-filled bag of thin tissue called the **amniotic sac** (am nee AHT ik) develops around the embryo. The sac continues to grow in size as the embryo grows. Inside the sac, the embryo floats in amniotic fluid.

Placenta The attachment holding the embryo to the wall of the uterus develops into a structure called the **placenta.** Within the placenta, oxygen and nutrients move from the mother's blood into tiny blood vessels that lead to the embryo. Dangerous substances can pass from mother to embryo, too, including alcohol, drugs, the chemicals in tobacco smoke, and some microscopic organisms that cause disease. Any of these substances can seriously harm the developing embryo.

Go Online
PHSchool.com

For: More on development before birth
Visit: PHSchool.com
Web Code: ctd-6191

Connect to YOUR LIFE Why do you think pregnant women are cautioned to avoid eating raw fish?

Umbilical Cord   About 25 days after fertilization, a ropelike structure called the **umbilical cord** (um BIL ih kul) develops between the embryo and the placenta. The umbilical cord is the embryo's lifeline. Blood vessels in the umbilical cord carry nutrients and oxygen from the placenta to the embryo and wastes from the embryo to the placenta.

The Growing Embryo   During the first two months of development, the major body systems and organs start to form in the embryo. For example, a basic heart, major blood vessels, kidneys, and endocrine glands develop. By the end of eight weeks, the embryo is about an inch long and has recognizable external features such as eyes, ears, arms, and legs. The head is large in proportion to the body—it makes up nearly 50 percent of the length of the embryo.

The Fetus   From the start of the third month until birth, the developing human is called a **fetus.** During the third to sixth month, the fetus begins to move and kick, a sign that its skeleton and muscles are developing. As its nervous system matures, the sense organs begin to function. The fetus becomes sensitive to light and sound and alternates periods of activity with periods of sleep.

From the seventh to the ninth month, the fetus continues to grow and develop. The size of the body increases so that it is more in proportion to the size of the head, and body fat accumulates. The eyelids open and close. By the end of the ninth month, the fetus is ready to be born.

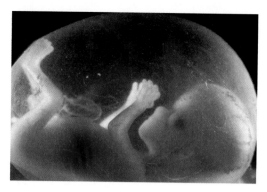

▲ **Fetus at 3 months**

▼ **Fetus at 8 months**

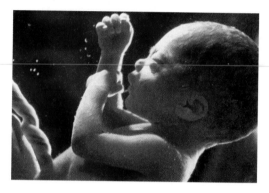

FIGURE 6   Between the third and eighth month of development, the facial features and limbs of a fetus change dramatically.

Section 2 Review

Key Ideas and Vocabulary

1. What happens during the first week of human development?
2. What happens during **implantation**?
3. What three structures protect and nourish the embryo, and later the fetus?
4. What is the **placenta**? What is its function?
5. How does a **fetus** change between the third and sixth months of pregnancy?

Critical Thinking

6. Calculating   Suppose that only 200 sperm out of the original 400 million sperm deposited in the vagina survive the journey to the egg. What percentage is this? **MATH**

Health and Community

Support for New Parents   Many communities offer free support groups for new parents. At the support group, parents can share the joys and frustrations of caring for their newborn. They may also learn new skills, such as how to bathe, diaper, and give first aid to their baby. Find out what services your community offers and make a pamphlet for new parents. **WRITING**

7. Relating Cause and Effect   Why is it an unhealthy decision for a pregnant woman to drink alcohol?
8. Sequencing   List in order the following steps of development: eyelids open and close, legs kick, embryo is about an inch long, amniotic sac develops.

Pregnancy

Objectives

▶ **Identify** four behaviors that are essential for a healthy pregnancy.

▶ **Explain** the importance of prenatal care throughout pregnancy.

▶ **Describe** the risks associated with teen pregnancy.

Vocabulary

• prenatal care
• obstetrician
• trimester
• ultrasound
• chorionic villus sampling
• amniocentesis
• ectopic pregnancy
• miscarriage
• preeclampsia
• gestational diabetes

Warm-Up •

Myth A pregnant woman doesn't need to visit the doctor until she begins to show, or look pregnant.

Fact Regular doctor visits from the beginning of pregnancy until the birth of the baby are recommended to ensure health.

WRITING List some other do's and don'ts for pregnant women. Review and update your list when you complete this section.

Staying Healthy During Pregnancy

Amanda starts her day with a bowl of oatmeal. Later, she and her husband go out for a brisk walk. At night, she skips a party where people will be smoking.

Amanda and her husband are thinking about having a baby. Even before she becomes pregnant, Amanda has started taking extra care to have a healthy pregnancy. **Getting proper nutrition and exercise and avoiding drugs and environmental hazards are especially important both before and throughout pregnancy.**

Proper Nutrition "Now you're eating for two," people sometimes say to pregnant women. This is because a pregnant woman needs to eat more calories to support the growth of her own body and the developing embryo or fetus. During pregnancy, a woman needs to consume about 300 extra calories a day. The best way to obtain these extra calories is to eat a well-balanced diet rich in the key nutrients listed in Figure 7.

One vitamin that is especially important during pregnancy is folic acid, or folate. Folic acid is essential for proper development of an embryo's neural tube, which later develops into the spinal cord and brain. The neural tube forms early in an embryo's development, often before a woman knows she is pregnant. Therefore, a woman should not wait until she knows she is pregnant to get enough folic acid. Doctors recommend that all women of childbearing age consume at least 0.4 mg (400 micrograms) of folic acid every day.

Exercise   Regular physical activity is also important for a healthy pregnancy. A fit woman will better meet the extra energy demands of carrying the fetus. She also reduces her risk for diabetes and other health problems during pregnancy. A woman should get her doctor's approval for her exercise program. Some forms of exercise should be avoided—for example, horseback riding, where there is a high risk of falling.

Avoiding Alcohol and Other Drugs   As soon as she plans to become pregnant, a woman should abstain from all alcohol, tobacco, and any other drugs not prescribed or approved by her doctor. These substances, even in small amounts, can harm or kill the developing baby, decrease the newborn's chance to live, or cause lifelong problems.

For example, women who drink alcohol during pregnancy risk having a baby with fetal alcohol syndrome. Symptoms of fetal alcohol syndrome may include mental retardation, minor to severe heart defects, and delayed growth. Drug use during pregnancy can also lead to a baby having low birthweight, or weighing less than 5.5 pounds at birth. These babies face an increased risk of health problems as newborns and throughout life.

Some drugs that are typically safe outside of pregnancy can cause harm to a fetus. A pregnant woman should talk to her doctor before using any prescription drugs or over-the-counter drugs, including pain medications, creams and lotions, and vitamins. Likewise, a woman should get her doctor's approval before drinking herbal teas or using other herbs.

Connect to YOUR LIFE   Which recommendations for pregnant women are also good everyday advice for yourself?

FIGURE 7   Proper nutrition contributes to the healthy development of a baby. **Reading Tables**   Name three nutrients that play a role in the development of the nervous system.

Important Nutrients During Pregnancy

Nutrient	Needed For
Folic acid	Formation of neural tube; brain and spinal cord development
Protein	Muscle formation and growth
Calcium	Bone and tooth formation; nerve and muscle development
Iron	Oxygen delivery by blood cells
Vitamin A	Cell and bone growth; eye development
Vitamin B complex	Nervous system development

Avoiding Environmental Hazards Some common substances found in the environment, including many chemicals and disease-causing organisms, can seriously harm a fetus. Pregnant women should take care to avoid exposure to these substances.

▶ **X-rays** The radiation from X-rays can harm a developing embryo or fetus. This is why doctors and dentists ask women if they could possibly be pregnant before taking an X-ray.

▶ **Lead** The main source of exposure to lead is from lead-based paint present in older homes. If a pregnant woman lives in a home built before 1978, she should contact her state health department for information on getting her home tested for lead.

▶ **Mercury** Most exposure to this dangerous metal comes from eating contaminated fish. Pregnant women should eat commercially caught fish only once a week, and should not eat swordfish or shark.

▶ **Cat Litter** Cat feces can contain a parasite that is especially dangerous to a developing fetus. Pregnant women should avoid contacting soiled cat litter or garden soil.

FIGURE 8 A doctor monitors the health of the mother-to-be and the fetus during regular prenatal visits.

Prenatal Care

A woman also needs to plan for **prenatal care,** or medical care during her pregnancy. Her doctor visits should be under the supervision of an **obstetrician,** a doctor who specializes in pregnancy and childbirth. **The chances of having a healthy baby greatly increase if the mother visits her doctor or clinic for regular checkups throughout pregnancy.**

The Three Trimesters A pregnancy is divided into three periods of time—**trimesters**—each of which is approximately three months long. Figure 8 lists things the parents-to-be can expect at routine visits.

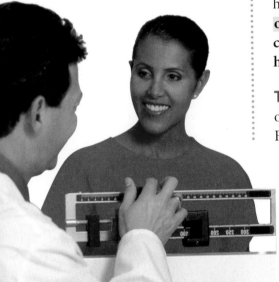

First Trimester

- Record medical history and weight
- Note conditions that could affect the pregnancy
- Prescribe prenatal vitamins as needed

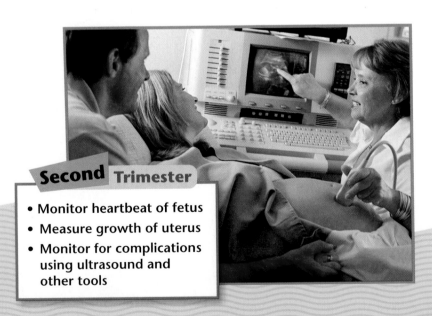

Second Trimester

- Monitor heartbeat of fetus
- Measure growth of uterus
- Monitor for complications using ultrasound and other tools

Monitoring Tools   Prenatal care gives a pregnant woman access to the latest medical tests and technologies.

▶ **Ultrasound** Did you know that your first pictures may have been taken months before you were born? High-frequency sound waves, or **ultrasound,** are used in most pregnancies to create an image of the developing fetus. Ultrasound may be used at any point during pregnancy, although it is typically used in the sixteenth to twentieth week. Using ultrasound, a doctor can tell the age of the fetus, whether it is a boy or girl, and if the heart, muscles, and bones are developing normally. Ultrasound may also detect the presence of more than one fetus or confirm the position of the fetus in the uterus.

▶ **Chorionic Villus Sampling** Around the eighth week of pregnancy, some women will undergo a test called **chorionic villus sampling,** or CVS. To perform the test, the doctor removes and tests a small piece of the developing placenta. CVS can detect inherited disorders in the embryo such as hemophilia or extra chromosomes. The test is only done when risk factors are present, such as a family history of genetic disorders or when the mother is over the age of 35. An older mother has an increased risk of having a baby with Down syndrome or other chromosomal abnormalities.

▶ **Amniocentesis** Another test that may be done around the fourteenth to sixteenth week of pregnancy is **amniocentesis** (am nee oh sen TEE sis). The procedure involves inserting a needle into the woman's abdomen and uterus to remove a small amount of amniotic fluid surrounding the fetus. The doctor then tests fetal cells naturally found in this fluid for abnormalities. Like CVS, amniocentesis is only performed when the fetus is at higher risk for a genetic disorder. CVS and amniocentesis are not routine tests because they slightly increase the risk of miscarriage, or death of the fetus.

Connect to YOUR LIFE Have you ever seen an ultrasound picture of a fetus? What features could you recognize?

Third Trimester
- Check position and size of fetus
- Check for warning signs of premature, or early, birth
- Continue to monitor for complications
- Discuss birth process

For: Updates on pregnancy care

Visit: www.SciLinks.org/health

Web Code: ctn-6192

Complications Problems can occur anytime during pregnancy. For some of these complications, timely treatment can reduce negative consequences or even save the life of the woman or fetus.

▶ **Ectopic Pregnancy** In the very rare case of an **ectopic pregnancy,** the blastocyst implants in the fallopian tube or elsewhere in the abdomen, instead of in the uterus. The embryo cannot develop normally and may put the mother's life at risk. Surgery is necessary to remove the embryo and repair the damaged fallopian tube.

▶ **Miscarriage** The death of an embryo or fetus in the first 20 weeks of pregnancy is called a **miscarriage.** Over 20 percent of pregnancies end in miscarriage. Miscarriage almost always occurs during the first trimester, sometimes before a woman knows she is pregnant. Miscarriage is usually caused by a serious genetic defect, but is sometimes due to illness or a drug the mother has taken. In other cases, there is no apparent reason for a miscarriage.

▶ **Preeclampsia** Also called toxemia, **preeclampsia** (pree ih KLAMP see uh) is characterized by high blood pressure, swelling of the wrists and ankles, and high levels of protein in the urine. Its onset is usually in the second or third trimester. Preeclampsia prevents the fetus from getting enough oxygen. This serious condition is treated with bed rest or medication.

▶ **Gestational Diabetes** Diabetes that develops in pregnant women is called **gestational diabetes,** and is marked by high blood sugar levels. Like preeclampsia, it usually develops later in pregnancy. If left untreated, excess blood sugar that passes through the placenta to the fetus may cause the fetus to grow too big. This increases the risk of a difficult birth, as well as breathing problems and obesity in the newborn.

▶ **Premature Birth** Delivery of a live baby before the 37th week of pregnancy is called premature birth. The earlier the birth, the more problems the baby tends to have. The lungs of a premature baby are usually not fully developed, and in some cases, the baby cannot breathe without help. A premature baby may receive care in an incubator, a chamber designed to protect the baby while he or she develops more.

FIGURE 9 A premature baby may need extended hospital care while his or her lungs and other organs continue to develop.

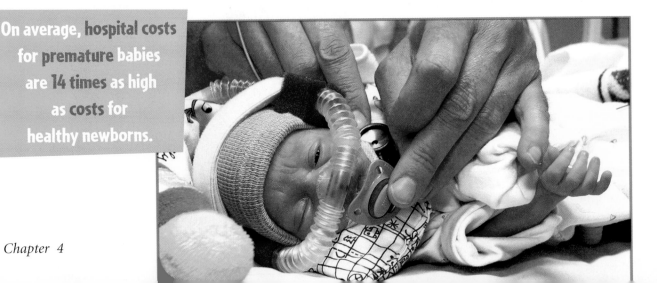

On average, hospital costs for premature babies are 14 times as high as costs for healthy newborns.

Teen Pregnancy

Each year in the United States, more than 800,000 girls between the ages of 15 and 19 become pregnant. Almost another 20,000 girls under the age of 15 become pregnant. The vast majority of teenage pregnancies are unwanted. Why, then, is the number so high?

Some teens who choose not to be abstinent lack accurate information about birth control. Some teens believe myths rather than facts about birth control or do not follow directions carefully. Still others do not use birth control because they think, "it can't happen to me." By risking an unplanned pregnancy, teens place their futures in jeopardy.

Facing a Pregnancy A teen who finds that she is pregnant faces some tough decisions. She needs to consider her feelings, values, and circumstances, as well as those of the father and others close to her. Talking things over with a parent or another close relative, friends, a member of the clergy, or a counselor may help her understand her thoughts and concerns.

Health Risks An unplanned pregnancy is an overwhelming experience at any age, but it is even more so for teenagers. **Pregnant teens face risks to their health and to the health of the fetus that most pregnant women in their 20s and 30s do not face.** For example, young teens are more likely to experience preeclampsia and premature birth.

There are many reasons why teens are more likely to experience complications during pregnancy.

▶ Teens are still growing and maturing. A teen's body may not be ready to support a developing baby.

▶ Many pregnant teens do not follow diets that provide adequate nutrition for both the baby and their own growing bodies.

▶ Pregnant teens are less likely than adult women to seek early prenatal care.

Babies of teenage mothers are also more likely to suffer health problems include low birthweight, birth defects, and delayed development. Getting adequate prenatal care throughout the pregnancy increases a teen's chance of having a healthy child.

Babies born to teen mothers are at increased risk for low birthweight.

FIGURE 10 Because teens are still maturing physically, a teen's body may not be ready to support a developing baby. Babies born to teen mothers are at risk for many health problems.

 Connect to YOUR LIFE **How would you give emotional support to a friend who became pregnant?**

Hands-On Activity

Be a Parent for a Day

Materials
5-pound bag of flour
plastic bag with tie

Try This

1. Place the bag of flour inside the plastic bag and fasten it shut. For the next 24 hours, you will be responsible for your bag of flour as if it were a real baby.

2. Choose a name for your "baby."

3. Follow these rules for taking care of your "baby."

   - Every 5 hours, including at night, feed your "baby" for 20 minutes. During this time, you must remain seated in one place and devote your full attention to your "baby."

   - Every 3 hours during the time that you are awake, allow 5 minutes for changing your "baby's" diaper.

   - Spend 15 minutes in the evening talking or reading to your "baby."

   - Never leave your "baby" alone. If necessary, arrange for someone to babysit.

Think and Discuss

1. How did being a parent of a bag of flour affect your lifestyle?

2. In what ways is a bag of flour an appropriate object to use to represent a baby?

3. When do you think is the best time for a person to become a parent? Explain.

Being a Teen Parent Teenagers who decide to raise their children need to think about the help they will receive from other people in their lives. Some teen fathers want to be an important part of their child's life. Often, however, teen fathers are not any more prepared to take on parenthood than are teen mothers. If teen parents do stay together or marry, they often must leave school and have difficulty finding a decent job and an affordable place to live.

Many teen parents turn to their own parents for help. Some families are willing to take on some of this responsibility. However, not all families are able or willing to help. As a result, many teen parents find that they must figure out how to live on their own.

For anyone, being a parent can be stressful. For teens, this is especially true because they often lack the skills and experience needed to be good parents. Some communities have parent-training programs that teach parenting skills. These programs also provide a place for young parents to seek support when problems arise.

Adoption   Some pregnant teens decide that adoption is the best choice for themselves and their babies. Adoption is a process by which a child becomes the legal responsibility of a parent or parents who are not the child's biological parents. An adoption should be handled by a public agency or a licensed private agency. This will help ensure that a child is adopted into a loving and financially secure home.

Deciding to give up a baby is difficult. It is normal for parents to wonder about the child for a long time after the adoption. Sharing these feelings with a counselor or other trusted individual can help a person cope with this difficult decision.

Ending a Pregnancy   One of the options available to a pregnant teen who feels she cannot go through with the pregnancy is to end the pregnancy through abortion. Abortion is the medical termination of a pregnancy. The procedure is safest when it is performed within the first twelve weeks of pregnancy.

When deciding about whether to have an abortion, a woman of any age should seek counseling and accurate information. A teen may also need permission from a parent, legal guardian, or judge before the abortion can proceed.

Abortion is a highly controversial issue. Some people think that abortion is wrong and should be illegal. Others think that abortion should be legal, but be more restricted. Still others think that abortion is a personal decision that should remain legal.

Section 3 Review

Key Ideas and Vocabulary

1. List four healthy habits that a pregnant woman should adopt before and during pregnancy.
2. Why is prenatal care so important throughout pregnancy?
3. About how long is each **trimester** of a pregnancy?
4. What is **chorionic villus sampling**? Under what conditions is it sometimes recommended?
5. Describe three symptoms of **preeclampsia**. How is it treated?
6. Explain why a pregnant teen faces more health risks during pregnancy than a mature woman.

Health at Home

Ultrasound Pictures Ask your mother or other relative with children if she saved any ultrasound pictures from her pregnancy. Ask permission to see the pictures. Ask about her emotions during the ultrasound—was she scared, happy, excited? Write a paragraph about the pictures and the mother's experience. **WRITING**

Critical Thinking

7. **Evaluating** From the following list, which food choices are *not* generally recommended for pregnant women: swordfish, spinach, herbal tea, wine, dairy products?
8. **Comparing and Contrasting** How are chorionic villus sampling and amniocentesis alike? How are they different?

Preventing Pregnancy

Objectives

▶ **Explain** why abstinence is the only completely effective way to prevent pregnancy and STIs.

▶ **Explain** why contraception is a responsible decision for those who choose to be sexually active.

▶ **Identify** the three general types of contraception.

Vocabulary

- contraception
- effectiveness
- failure rate
- spermicide
- sterilization

Warm-Up

Dear Advice Line,

My friends seem to think they know a lot about birth control, but I really don't think I should trust their advice. Where can I go to find reliable information about birth control?

WRITING Write a response to this teen with advice about where to find reliable information about birth control.

Abstinence

The only way for a person to eliminate the risks of pregnancy and sexually transmitted infections is to practice abstinence. Many teens feel that abstinence is the best decision for them at this point in their lives. Teens choose abstinence for a number of reasons.

▶ They think that sexual intimacy should be reserved for a long-term committed relationship, such as marriage.

▶ They do not feel ready to take on the added responsibilities that come with a sexually intimate relationship.

▶ They want to keep their focus on achieving current goals such as athletics or getting into college.

▶ They want to be certain to avoid pregnancy and sexually transmitted infections.

Choosing sexual abstinence does not mean avoiding intimate relationships. Abstinent couples have the opportunity to get to know each other on a deep emotional level and to develop a relationship based on understanding, caring, and trust.

Connect to YOUR LIFE What other good reasons can you think of for choosing abstinence?

Contraception

Contraception, or birth control, is the use of an appropriate method to intentionally prevent pregnancy. There is a wide array of different contraceptive methods. **Couples who choose to be sexually active, but do not wish to have a child, must decide on a method of contraception that is right for them.** Many factors should be considered when choosing a contraceptive method.

▶ Can the method be purchased over the counter or is a prescription required?

▶ How much planning and preparation is needed?

▶ Does the product have health risks or side effects?

▶ Does the method protect against STIs, including HIV? If so, which STIs does it protect against?

▶ How effective is the method at preventing pregnancy?

Effectiveness   The **effectiveness** of a contraceptive method is the likelihood that using the method will prevent pregnancy. Often, the effectiveness of a contraceptive method is measured by its **failure rate,** the percentage of pregnancies that result in one year in a group of people who use that method. The lower the failure rate, the higher the effectiveness.

Many factors contribute to a method's effectiveness. Sometimes a failure occurs through no fault of the couple. More often, however, a failure occurs because the couple did not follow instructions or didn't use the method *every time* they had intercourse. Figure 17 on page 82 compares the failure rates for the methods discussed in this section.

Getting More Information   People who are sexually active need accurate information and advice about contraception. If possible, the best way to get advice is to ask a parent or another trusted adult. Doctors, other healthcare professionals, and counselors at family planning clinics are also reliable sources of information.

FIGURE 11 When seeking information about birth control, it is important to talk with an informed person who can be trusted, such as your doctor.

Barrier Methods

Most contraceptive methods fall into one of three categories—barrier methods, hormonal methods, and permanent methods. Barrier methods prevent sperm from reaching an egg. Some methods, such as condoms, diaphragms, cervical caps, shields, and sponges, are physical barriers. Others, such as spermicide, are chemical barriers.

People who use condoms
- should NOT use teeth to tear open the package.
- should NOT keep condoms in a car or wallet.
- should NOT use a condom after the expiration date.

Male Condom   One form of contraception that can be purchased over the counter is the male condom. The male condom is a thin sheath that fits over an erect penis. Condoms prevent pregnancy by stopping sperm from being released into the vagina.

Condoms are made of latex, polyurethane, or animal intestine. While all of these types can prevent pregnancy, latex condoms provide the best protection against STIs. Even latex condoms, however, do not provide protection from all types of STIs. See Chapter 5 for more information.

Some condoms contain a **spermicide,** a chemical agent that kills sperm. Because spermicide may increase the risk of HIV transmission, the Centers for Disease Control and Prevention (CDC) recommends the use of condoms *without* spermicide.

Condoms must be used carefully and consistently to prevent pregnancy and the transmission of STIs.

▶ Condoms must be rolled over an erect penis before any penetration of the vagina occurs.

▶ If the condom does not have a reservoir tip to collect semen, a small space—about one-half inch—should be left between the tip of the penis and the condom.

▶ The male should withdraw while the penis is still erect. As he withdraws, he should hold the rim of the condom at the base of the penis.

▶ A condom cannot be reused. It should be discarded immediately.

▶ Condoms should not be exposed to heat, lotions, or petroleum-based products, which weaken latex.

Female Condom   The female condom, which is available over the counter, is a plastic sheath that is inserted into the vagina. It is held in place by two flexible rings. One ring covers the cervix. The other ring remains outside of the vagina. Like the male condom, a female condom can only be used once. Although the female condom does provide some protection from STIs, it does not provide the same level of protection as the male condom.

FIGURE 13   The female condom lines the inside of the vagina and forms a barrier that prevents sperm from entering the woman's body.

▲ **Diaphragm**   ▲ **Cervical Cap**   ▲ **Shield**

FIGURE 14 These devices block sperm from reaching the cervix, while the spermicide applied to them acts to kill the sperm.

The Diaphragm, Cap, and Shield Three barrier contraceptive methods that are available only by prescription are the diaphragm, cervical cap, and shield. All three devices cover the cervix and block sperm from entering the uterus.

The diaphragm and cervical cap are dome-shaped cups made of soft rubber or latex. The cervical cap is smaller than the diaphragm. A female must see her healthcare professional to be measured for the proper-sized diaphragm or cervical cap. After a weight gain or weight loss of 10 pounds or more, or a pregnancy, she should be fitted again.

A shield, which is made of silicone, has a valve that helps keep the device in place. The shield comes in only one size.

The diaphragm, cap, and shield share some similarities.

▶ The devices do *not* protect against STIs.

▶ Spermicide must be applied to them before they are inserted.

▶ They must remain in place for the recommended amount of time after intercourse (usually 6 to 8 hours) to prevent pregnancy.

▶ To avoid infection, they should be removed within the instructed amount of time.

▶ They can be washed and stored for repeated use.

The Sponge The sponge is a disk-shaped, foam device that contains spermicide. Sponges can be purchased over the counter. Before intercourse, the sponge is moistened with water and then inserted into the vagina. After intercourse, the sponge should be left in place for at least six hours but not more than 30 hours. Sponges are thrown away after use. The sponge does *not* protect against STIs.

Spermicides Although spermicides can be used alone as a contraceptive method, it is recommended that they be used in conjunction with another more reliable method. Foams, jellies, and creams are three types of spermicide products. They are inserted into the vagina with an applicator. Insertion should occur no more than 30 minutes before intercourse.

A contraceptive suppository is a small capsule that contains spermicide. It must be inserted into the vagina 10 to 15 minutes before intercourse so that it has time to dissolve. Spermicides do *not* protect against STIs.

▲ Oral contraceptives

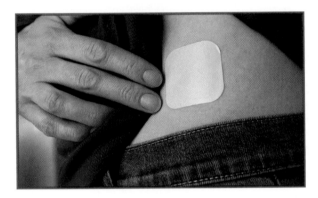
▲ Skin patch

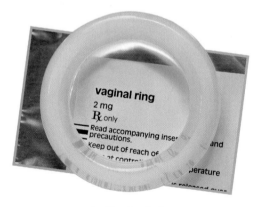
▲ Vaginal ring

FIGURE 15 Hormonal methods are highly effective, but cause more side effects than other methods. The side effects usually subside after a few months.

Hormonal Methods

Hormonal methods of contraception work by preventing ovulation or inhibiting fertilization. Currently, the only available hormonal methods are for females and require a prescription. All of these methods are more effective than barrier methods, but users are more likely to experience side effects. Hormonal methods do *not* protect against STIs.

Oral Contraceptives ("The Pill") Oral contraceptives usually come in packs of 28 pills. A female takes one pill each day, regardless of how often she has intercourse. If she forgets to take a hormone-containing pill for one or more days, a back-up contraceptive may have to be used for a period of time. Oral contraceptives come in two general forms.

▶ **Combination Pill** The combination pill contains synthetic versions of the female hormones estrogen and progestin (a hormone that is similar to progesterone). The hormones prevent ovulation—that is, they prevent the ovaries from releasing eggs. Side effects of estrogen-containing pills may include dizziness, nausea, and changes in menstruation. Rarely, users may experience cardiovascular problems such as high blood pressure and blood clots.

▶ **Mini Pill** The mini pill contains only progestin and may not prevent ovulation. Instead, it causes the mucus around the cervix to thicken. The thick mucus prevents sperm from reaching an egg. The mini pill is often prescribed to females who experience side effects from estrogen or who are breastfeeding.

Patches Another hormonal method is a skin patch, which is worn on the lower abdomen, buttocks, or upper body. The patch prevents ovulation by releasing estrogen and progestin through the skin. The patch is changed once a week. Patch users may have a higher risk of blood clots than combined pill users.

Rings The vaginal ring is a flexible ring containing hormones that a female inserts into her vagina. The walls of the vagina hold the ring in place. The ring is worn for three weeks and then removed while the female has her menstrual period. At the end of the fourth week, a new ring is inserted.

Injections A female may also receive an injection of progestin every three months. It is recommended that a female does not receive injections for more than two years in a row due to a risk of bone loss.

Permanent Methods

Permanent methods of contraception are only appropriate for people who are sure that they either do not want any children or do not want more children. Sterilization is the use of surgery or other procedures to make a person incapable of reproduction. Sterilization does *not* protect against STIs. Because sterilization makes it no longer possible for a person to have children, it is a major life decision. Sometimes these procedures can be reversed with another surgery, but the chances are unlikely.

Vasectomy   A male can be sterilized by a procedure called a vasectomy. A doctor makes a small incision in the scrotum and then severs each vas deferens, the tubes that carry sperm from the testes. The male still releases semen during ejaculation, but after four to six weeks the semen does not contain sperm.

Tubal Ligation   The most common method of sterilization for females is called tubal ligation. During this procedure, a woman's fallopian tubes are cut or closed, blocking sperm's access to a released egg.

Sterilization Implant   Another sterilization option for a female is to have a small, coiled implant inserted in each fallopian tube. Scar tissue forms around the implants, blocking the passageway of eggs and sperm. Unlike tubal ligation, this method does not require an incision. Neither method affects a woman's sexual function or menstrual cycle.

FIGURE 16   During sterilization, each vas deferens in males or each fallopian tube in females is altered. The sperm or eggs are no longer able to travel their normal path.

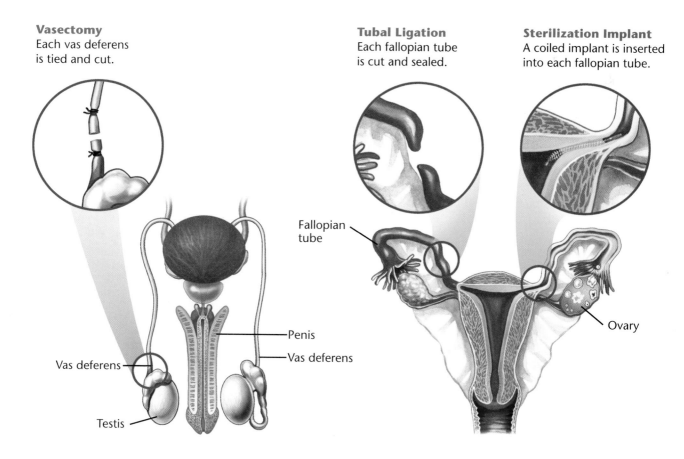

Vasectomy
Each vas deferens is tied and cut.

Tubal Ligation
Each fallopian tube is cut and sealed.

Sterilization Implant
A coiled implant is inserted into each fallopian tube.

Fallopian tube

Penis

Vas deferens

Vas deferens

Testis

Ovary

FIGURE 17 When deciding on a contraceptive method, a person should carefully evaluate the effectiveness of each option.

Effectiveness of Contraceptive Methods

Contraceptive Method	Failure Rate*	Protection from STIs	Availability	Proper Use
Abstinence	0%	Complete		
Male condom	11%	Some	Over the counter	Applied immediately before intercourse; used once
Female condom	21%	Limited	Over the counter	Inserted before intercourse; used once
Diaphragm plus spermicide	17%	None	Prescription	Must be left in place for 6 hours after intercourse; can be washed and reused
Cervical cap plus spermicide	17 to 23%	None	Prescription	Proper insertion can be difficult; must be left in place for 8 hours after intercourse; can be washed and reused
Shield plus spermicide	15%	None	Prescription	Must be left in place for 8 hours after intercourse; can be washed and reused
Sponge	16%	None	Over the counter	Must be left in place for 6 hours after intercourse; discarded after use
Spermicide alone	35%	None	Over the counter	Varies based on type
Combination pill or Mini pill	1 to 2%	None	Prescription	Must be taken daily
Patch	1 to 2%	None	Prescription	New patch applied once a week
Ring	1 to 2%	None	Prescription	New ring inserted once a month
Injection	<1%	None	Prescription	One injection every three months
Permanent methods	<1%	None	Medical procedure	One-time procedure

* These approximate failure rates represent the percentage of women who become pregnant during the first year of using a method. The rates for the diaphragm, cap, shield, and sponge apply to women who have never been pregnant. These devices are more likely to fail in women who have been pregnant.

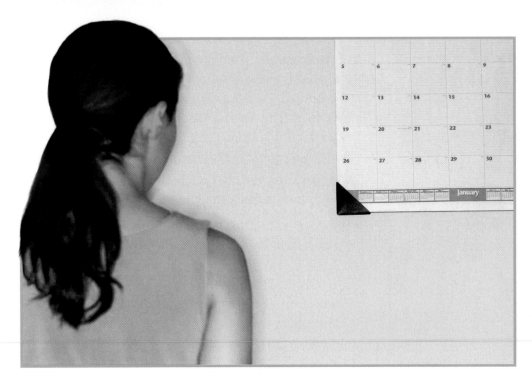

FIGURE 18 Periodic abstinence is a contraceptive method best used by adult couples who do not want to use barrier or hormonal birth control methods.
Comparing and Contrasting Why is periodic abstinence an unreliable method of contraception for teens?

Unreliable Methods

To ensure the prevention of pregnancy, it is important that couples understand how and why the efffective methods of contraception work. Unfortunately, even when information about effective methods of birth control is available, some people use methods that do not work. **Knowing why unreliable methods are ineffective can help a person separate inaccurate information from accurate information.**

Periodic Abstinence Couples who practice periodic abstinence abstain from intercourse during the days of the female's cycle when she is likely to become pregnant. This method is also known as natural family planning or fertility awareness.

To practice periodic abstinence, a woman must pay careful attention to the days of her cycle. Some women also monitor symptoms such as body temperature, the color of cervical mucus, and breast tenderness to predict when they will ovulate. Several factors can decrease a woman's ability to make accurate predictions about her menstrual cycle.

▶ sickness or medications

▶ emotional stress

▶ alcohol or tobacco use

▶ change in sleep cycle

For careful and attentive women with predictable menstrual cycles, periodic abstinence can be as effective as barrier methods. However, periodic abstinence is *not* reliable for adolescents. It can take many years for a female's cycle to become regular enough for her to accurately predict when she will ovulate during each cycle. Also, periodic abstinence does *not* protect against STIs.

FIGURE 19 Couples who fail to make decisions together about reliable contraception may face an unplanned pregnancy.

Withdrawal   One method that is unreliable for anyone is withdrawal, sometimes called "coitus interruptus." Withdrawal is the removal of the penis from the vagina just before ejaculation. Withdrawal is not effective for preventing pregnancy for a couple of reasons.

▶ A male may not always have the self-control to withdraw before ejaculation.

▶ Before ejaculation, some fluid that may contain sperm is released from the penis. The male has no way of knowing when this fluid may be released. Therefore, even if he successfully withdraws before ejaculation, pregnancy can still occur.

Withdrawal also does *not* protect against STIs.

Other Unreliable Methods   Females who use douching as a form of birth control hope that the douching will kill or wash the sperm out of the vagina. Sperm, however, can go through the cervix and enter the uterus just seconds after ejaculation. Douching, in fact, may help propel the sperm into the uterus.

Urinating after unprotected intercourse has no effect on preventing pregnancy. Urine flows through the urethra, but sperm are ejaculated into the vagina. Therefore, urine does not wash away or kill sperm.

Section 4 Review

Key Ideas and Vocabulary

1. Explain why abstinence is the only 100 percent effective way to prevent pregnancy and STIs.
2. List five factors a couple should consider when choosing a contraceptive method.
3. What does the term **effectiveness** mean in reference to a contraceptive method?
4. Describe how barrier, hormonal, and permanent methods of contraception work. Give one example of each method.
5. What is a **spermicide?** What other methods of contraception should be used with a spermicide?

Health at School

Comparing Contraceptives Create a poster that compares five of the contraceptive methods you learned about in this chapter. Include abstinence as one of the five methods compared. Be sure to include each method's effectiveness and its ability to prevent the spread of STIs. **WRITING**

Critical Thinking

6. **Applying Concepts** What is the only method of contraception that also offers some protection against STIs?
7. **Comparing and Contrasting** Compare the pros and cons of barrier methods and hormonal methods.

Discovery EDUCATION

TEENS Talk

Teen Pregnancy Describe how pregnancy affected the long-term plans of the teens in the video.

Reviewing Key Ideas

Section 1

1. Which of the following is NOT a part of a successful marriage?
   a. compatibility
   b. compromise
   c. perfectionism
   d. communication

2. Explain the importance of commitment in a successful marriage.

3. Describe two big challenges most married teenagers face.

4. **Critical Thinking** Discuss at least three factors that a couple should consider before they decide to be parents.

Section 2

5. During implantation
   a. the egg is fertilized.
   b. the blastocyst travels to the uterus.
   c. the blastocyst attaches to the wall of the uterus.
   d. the embryo grows to about an inch in length.

6. Describe how a fetus obtains nutrients and gets rid of wastes.

7. What changes occur in a fetus between the seventh and ninth month of development?

8. **Critical Thinking** Why do you think many expectant parents keep pregnancy a secret until after the first trimester?

Section 3

9. Which nutrient is critical for proper neural tube development?
   a. iron
   b. folic acid
   c. sodium
   d. vitamin A

10. List four environmental hazards of particular concern to pregnant women.

11. During which trimester of a pregnancy should a woman start prenatal care?

12. **Critical Thinking** Why do you think that many pregnant teens do not receive proper medical care during the first trimester?

Section 4

13. Which contraceptive method is most effective in preventing pregnancy and avoiding the transmission of STIs?
    a. a female condom
    b. a diaphragm
    c. oral contraception
    d. a male condom

14. List three benefits of sexual abstinence.

15. How does the combination pill prevent pregnancy?

16. Explain why withdrawal is an unreliable method of birth control.

17. **Critical Thinking** Why do you think that the use of alcohol or other drugs leads to many unplanned pregnancies?

Building Health Skills

18. **Advocacy** How could you help an older cousin stop smoking before she decides to have a baby?

19. **Making Decisions** Suppose you were recently married, but did not want to have children for several years. What factors would you consider when deciding how to delay parenthood?

20. **Setting Goals** Identify one habit you could change that would help you be a better parent in your 20s or 30s. It may seem a long way off, but changing habits is easiest when you are young. Write down the habit you would like to change, and monitor your progress over the school year.

Health and Community

Folic Acid Awareness Many health organizations recommend that all women increase their folic acid consumption, starting in their teen years. Create a public service announcement to deliver this important message to teenage girls. In it, describe the importance of folic acid and offer tips for adding more of it to one's diet. **WRITING**

Chapter 5

Sexually Transmitted Infections and AIDS

Go Online
PHSchool.com

Discovery EDUCATION™

TEENS Talk

CLASSROOM VIDEO #22

Risks and STIs

Preview Activity

How Risky Is Sexual Activity?

Complete this activity before you watch the video.

1. Complete each of the following statements by filling in the blank.
   a. Being sexually active as a teen is __?__.
   b. There are __?__ risks that come with sexual activity.
   c. A person should not be sexually active until __?__.

2. Look over your responses. In a paragraph, summarize what you learned about yourself by completing the statements. **WRITING**

365

The Risks of Sexual Activity

Objectives

▶ **List** risky behaviors associated with the current epidemic of sexually transmitted infections.

▶ **Identify** the best way to avoid sexually transmitted infections during the teen years.

Vocabulary

• sexually transmitted infection (STI)
• monogamy

Warm-Up ....

Quick Quiz Which of these statements do you think are true? Which are false?

① It can take only one sexual contact with an infected person to get a sexually transmitted infection.

② Even if you've been infected with a sexually transmitted infection before, you can get that same infection again.

③ You can have more than one sexually transmitted infection at a time.

④ You can get a sexually transmitted infection from sharing needles.

WRITING For each of your responses, explain why you gave the answer you did. Review your answers after reading this section.

The Silent Epidemic

Any pathogen that spreads from one person to another during sexual contact is called a **sexually transmitted infection,** or **STI.** (Such infections are sometimes called sexually transmitted diseases, or STDs.) There are 19 million new cases of STIs in the United States each year. Of those cases, over 3 million occur in people under age 20.

Harmful Effects of STIs The STI epidemic is a serious concern for several reasons. STIs are harmful in terms of physical and emotional suffering. And yearly healthcare expenses related to STIs in the United States amount to well over $10 billion.

In the short term, STIs may cause pain, discomfort, and embarrassment. The long-term consequences of STIs may include an increased risk of certain cancers and an increased risk of infertility in both men and women. Infertility is the condition of being unable to have children.

Many STIs can be treated with medicines, but some are incurable. If left untreated, some STIs are fatal. Unlike many other infectious diseases, people do not develop immunity to STIs after being infected. A person can be cured and then reinfected with the same STI again.

Risky Behaviors and the STI Epidemic There are several risky behaviors that account for the current STI epidemic, including ignoring the risks of sexual activity, having sexual contact with multiple partners, and not getting proper treatment when necessary.

For: Updates on sexually transmitted infections
Visit: www.SciLinks.org/health
Web Code: ctn-7221

▶ **Ignoring Risks** Being sexually active puts a person at risk for STIs. Many people who are sexually active do not take precautions against infection. They often do not realize the risks of contracting STIs, or they choose to ignore the risks. Adolescents in particular tend to ignore the risks, thinking "It can't happen to me." But the reality is that it can, and it does happen to many teens.

▶ **Multiple Partners** Many people begin to engage in sexual activity at a young age, and some may have multiple sexual partners during their lifetimes. The more sexual partners a person has, the greater the chance of getting an STI.

▶ **Not Seeking Treatment** Some people who become infected do not seek immediate medical treatment. Sometimes people are too embarrassed to seek treatment. Others don't know that they have an STI because they do not recognize the symptoms. In some cases, STIs have no symptoms and can only be detected by laboratory tests. Sometimes the symptoms go away temporarily, leading the person to think the infection has been cured. In all of these situations, the infection may go untreated, increasing the chances that the person will spread it to others.

Connect to YOUR LIFE What advice would you give a friend who seems to be ignoring the risks of sexual activity?

FIGURE 1 This graph shows data for one STI, chlamydia, that is common among young people. **Evaluating** Why do you think young people are especially at risk for STIs?

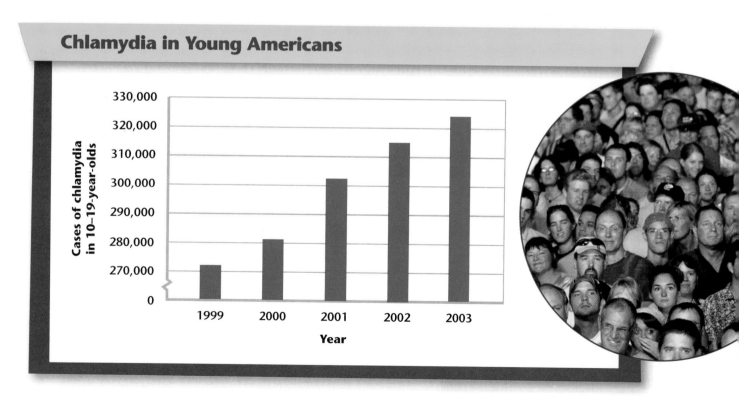

Chlamydia in Young Americans

Cases of chlamydia in 10–19-year-olds

- 330,000
- 320,000
- 310,000
- 300,000
- 290,000
- 280,000
- 270,000
- 0

Year: 1999, 2000, 2001, 2002, 2003

FIGURE 2 Educating yourself about STIs can help you make healthy decisions.

Avoiding STIs

STIs are transmitted mainly through sexual contact, but a few are also transmitted through contact with the blood of an infected person. **In the teen years, the best way to avoid STIs is to practice sexual abstinence and avoid drug abuse and other behaviors that may lead to exposure to infected blood or body fluids.**

Practice Abstinence   The most certain way to avoid STIs is to practice sexual abstinence. Sexual abstinence means not engaging in sexual activity. Sexual activity such as oral sex, anal sex, genital-to-genital touching, and intercourse can transmit STIs.

Oral sex is contact between a person's mouth and another person's genitals. Because oral sex can expose partners to skin sores and semen or vaginal fluids, there is a risk of transmitting STIs. Anal sex occurs when a male inserts his penis into his partner's anus. This is risky because the tissue in the anus can tear easily, exposing both partners to each other's blood or body fluids. Genital-to-genital touching, even without intercourse, can also transmit certain STIs that spread through sores in the skin.

Because sexual activity involves the risk of STI transmission, abstinence is the safest behavior for avoiding STIs. Teens who have not been abstinent in the past can reduce their risk by choosing to be abstinent in the future.

Avoid Drugs   Some STIs can be transmitted by blood-to-blood contact. People who share needles to inject illegal drugs or steroids run a high risk of contracting certain STIs. Individuals who get body piercings or tattoos also run a risk of being infected with a contaminated needle. Furthermore, anyone who engages in sexual activity with someone who has come into contact with an infected needle is at risk for STIs.

Drugs, including alcohol, also play an indirect role in the STI epidemic. Because alcohol and other drugs impair the ability to think clearly, people may make decisions they later regret.

Choose Responsible Friends A good way to ensure that you practice abstinence and avoid drugs is to choose friends who have also chosen those behaviors. Friends who support your healthy decisions can make it easier to resist the pressure to use drugs or engage in sexual behavior.

Sexual Fidelity in Marriage Sexual fidelity, also called **monogamy,** means that two people have sexual contact only with one another. In a long-term monogamous relationship, such as a marriage in which both partners are uninfected and are faithful to each other, there is little concern about STIs. Teens, however, should *not* count on sexual fidelity to protect them from STIs. This is because teen relationships are typically not stable or long lasting, although they might seem so at the time.

Barrier Protection For people who are sexually active, but not in a long-term monogamous relationship, the best way to reduce the risk of infection is to use a condom during every sexual encounter. A condom is a latex or polyurethane sheath that covers the penis. When used correctly, it acts as a physical barrier against many STIs. However, condoms do not provide 100% protection against any STI, and they do not provide any protection at all against some STIs. For example, some STIs can be spread by skin sores that are not covered by a condom. Or a condom could break during sexual activity. Abstinence remains the best protection against STIs.

FIGURE 3 Choosing friends and activities that encourage abstinence can greatly reduce your risk of becoming infected with an STI.

Section 1 Review

Key Ideas and Vocabulary

1. What is a **sexually transmitted infection**?
2. What are three risky behaviors that contribute to the current STI epidemic?
3. Explain how practicing abstinence, avoiding drugs, and your choice of friends can help you avoid STIs.
4. What is **monogamy?** How is it helpful in protecting against STIs?

Critical Thinking

5. Relating Cause and Effect How is the fact that some STIs have few or no symptoms related to the STI epidemic?

Health and Community

STI Education Create a poster or a web page to educate teens about the risks of sexual activity and STIs. Include statistics about the incidence of STIs in teens. Include other facts that you think teens should be aware of. WRITING

6. Evaluating Explain how refusal skills and effective communication are important skills that teens can use to avoid STIs.
7. Applying Concepts Describe how someone would most effectively avoid STIs throughout their lifetime.

Kinds of STIs

Objectives

▶ **Identify** three of the most common STIs, including their symptoms and treatments.

▶ **List** four other STIs and describe their symptoms.

▶ **Know** when a person should seek treatment for an STI.

Vocabulary

- trichomoniasis
- urethritis
- vaginitis
- human papilloma virus
- chlamydia
- pelvic inflammatory disease
- gonorrhea
- genital herpes
- syphilis
- chancre

Warm-Up

Myth All STIs can be treated with antibiotics.

Fact STIs caused by viruses cannot be treated with antibiotics. Antibiotics are only used to treat STIs caused by bacteria. Several STIs caused by viruses cannot be cured and can cause lifelong health problems.

WRITING Do you think most teens are aware that some STIs are not easily treated? And that some may persist for years? Explain your answer.

The Most Common STIs

Like other infectious diseases you have learned about, STIs are caused by pathogens, including bacteria, viruses, and protozoans. The pathogens that cause STIs live in the reproductive organs of males and females. Some also live in the blood. STIs can be spread from person to person through blood and body fluids such as semen, vaginal secretions, and breast milk.

Early diagnosis and treatment of STIs is essential in preventing long-term health problems. Although some STIs do not have obvious symptoms, many do have distinct symptoms. Anyone experiencing symptoms of an STI should see a doctor immediately.

Three of the most common STIs in the United States are trichomoniasis, human papilloma virus, and chlamydia. It is important to be able to recognize the symptoms of these infections.

Trichomoniasis The STI known as **trichomoniasis** (trik uh moh NY uh sis) is caused by a protozoan that infects the urinary tract or vagina. In males, symptoms include painful urination, a clear discharge from the penis, and some itching. Most males experience no symptoms at all. Symptoms in females include itching and burning in the vagina, an unpleasant-smelling, yellowish discharge, and pain when urinating.

A doctor can prescribe medicine to cure a trichomoniasis infection. In males, if trichomoniasis is not treated, it can lead to inflammation of the lining of the urethra, called **urethritis** (yoor uh THRY tis). In females, untreated trichomoniasis can lead to **vaginitis** (vaj uh NY tis), which is a vaginal infection or irritation.

Human Papilloma Virus   The most common viral STI in the United States is caused by the **human papilloma virus** (pap uh LOH muh), or HPV. In many cases, HPV causes no symptoms, so people may not be aware that they are infected.

Some forms of HPV cause genital warts, which may itch or burn. A doctor can remove the warts, but they may reappear. Sometimes, the body's immune system will destroy the virus, clearing the body of infection. But in some people, HPV remains in the body for life.

One of the most serious conditions associated with HPV infection is cervical cancer in women. Having regular Pap tests can help detect this type of cancer before it becomes life threatening.

Chlamydia   The most common STI caused by bacteria in the United States is **chlamydia** (kluh MID ee uh). People who are sexually active should be checked regularly for chlamydia. The infection can be cured with antibiotics.

Infected males often experience painful, frequent urination and discharge from the penis. If untreated, chlamydia may lead to urethritis.

In females, chlamydia often has no symptoms other than a yellowish vaginal discharge. If untreated, chlamydia can cause a serious infection of the reproductive organs called **pelvic inflammatory disease,** or PID. PID can lead to infertility or an ectopic pregnancy, a potentially fatal condition where a fertilized egg implants somewhere other than in the uterus. In addition, a pregnant woman can transmit chlamydia to her baby during birth. If an infected infant survives, it may suffer damage to the lungs or eyes.

Go Online
PHSchool.com

For: More on sexually transmitted infections
Visit: PHSchool.com
Web Code: ctd-7222

FIGURE 4   The micrographs show the pathogens that cause trichomoniasis, HPV, and chlamydia. These STIs affect millions of Americans every year.

Connect to YOUR LIFE   For each STI, list the symptoms that a person needs to watch for.

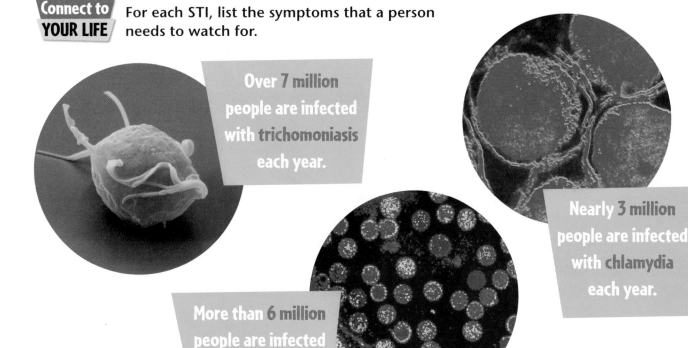

Over 7 million people are infected with trichomoniasis each year.

More than 6 million people are infected with HPV each year.

Nearly 3 million people are infected with chlamydia each year.

Other STIs

Other STIs can also cause health problems and require medical treatment. Information about some of these STIs is summarized in Figure 6. **Other STIs include hepatitis, gonorrhea, genital herpes, and syphilis.**

Hepatitis Hepatitis B and C, also called HBV and HCV, are sexually transmitted infections that attack the liver. They are also spread by blood-to-blood contact, such as when people share needles.

Individuals with HBV or HCV are often unaware of their infection. The most common symptoms are fatigue, abdominal pain, nausea, and jaundice. Both infections may lead to liver cancer or cirrhosis (sih ROH sis), a condition in which normal liver tissue is replaced by scar tissue.

Hepatitis B and C can be diagnosed by a blood test. Medications may relieve symptoms, but there is no cure for HBV or HCV. Children are now routinely vaccinated against HBV. Currently, there is no vaccine for HCV.

Gonorrhea A bacterial STI that infects the urinary tract of males and females and the reproductive organs of females is **gonorrhea** (gahn uh REE uh). Researchers estimate that more than 700,000 Americans are infected with gonorrhea each year. Males usually have a thick, puslike discharge from the penis and painful urination. Females sometimes experience painful urination and a puslike discharge from the vagina or urinary tract. More often, however, symptoms in a woman are very mild and may not be noticed. If left untreated, gonorrhea can lead to urethritis and infertility in males. In females it may lead to PID and infertility.

An infected woman can transmit gonorrhea to her baby during birth. In the United States, babies are given medicated eyedrops at birth to prevent infection of the eyes.

Because gonorrhea often has no noticeable symptoms, people participating in high-risk behaviors should get regular medical checkups. Treatment for gonorrhea requires antibiotics.

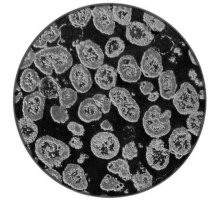

▲ **Gonorrhea**

FIGURE 5 Newborn babies are routinely given medicated eyedrops to prevent gonorrhea infection. The micrograph above shows the bacteria that cause gonorrhea.

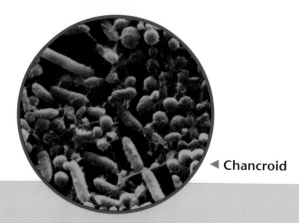
◀ Chancroid

FIGURE 6 Chancroid, bacterial vaginosis, pubic lice, and scabies are all treatable STIs. **Classifying** Which of these STIs can affect both males and females?

Other STIs

Infection	Pathogen	Symptoms	How Spread	Treatment
Chancroid	Bacteria	Painful sores around the genitals	Contact with sores	Antibiotics
Bacterial vaginosis	Bacteria	In women, discharge, pain, itching, or burning in or around the vagina	Role of sexual activity in the spread of bacterial vaginosis is unclear	Antibiotics
Pubic lice and Scabies	Insects and mites that infest the hair around the genitals	Itching around the genitals; a rash	Direct physical contact with an infested person or with infested clothing or bedding	Medicated shampoo; washing infested clothing or bedding in very hot water

Genital Herpes Another STI caused by a virus is **genital herpes** (HUR peez). The virus that causes genital herpes is the herpes simplex virus. Researchers estimate that one out of five people ages 12 and older is infected with a herpes simplex virus.

In some people, the symptoms may be hardly noticeable, and they may not realize they are infected. In other people, symptoms may be more severe, including painful blisters that appear on or around the genitals. A doctor can prescribe medicine to relieve the discomfort and dry up the blisters, but there is no cure for genital herpes. Infected people can experience periodic outbreaks of blisters throughout their lives.

An infected individual can pass the herpes simplex virus to a sexual partner whether blisters are present or not. A woman with genital herpes can infect her infant during childbirth, causing blindness and possibly death. A doctor may recommend that an infected woman have a cesarean section to prevent the baby from being infected.

▲ Pubic louse

Connect to YOUR LIFE If a friend were considering a body piercing, what would you say about the risk of hepatitis?

Syphilis Although far less common than it used to be, thousands of people in the United States become infected with syphilis each year. **Syphilis** (SIF uh lis) is a serious bacterial STI that progresses through three distinct stages.

▶ In the first stage, a painless sore called a **chancre** (SHANG kur) appears at the site of exposure. The bacteria may spread from the sore to different parts of the body.

▶ In the second stage, sores appear in the mouth and flulike symptoms develop. A nonitchy skin rash often appears on the hands and feet.

▶ In the third stage, symptoms may disappear for years. During this time, however, the bacteria attack internal parts of the body, such as the brain and heart. Eventually, untreated syphilis can cause brain damage, paralysis, and heart disease. This damage can lead to death.

In its early stages, syphilis can be treated and cured with antibiotics. Once it progresses beyond the second stage, the bacteria can be killed, but any damage that has already occurred is permanent.

A pregnant woman with syphilis will pass the disease to her developing baby. If the mother does not receive treatment during pregnancy, syphilis can damage the baby's skin, bones, eyes, teeth, and liver. A baby born with syphilis is said to have congenital syphilis.

FIGURE 7 An itchless rash on the hands is one of the symptoms of syphilis. The bacteria that cause syphilis are spiral-shaped, as you can see in the micrograph. The poster shown here was part of a public health program in the 1940s.

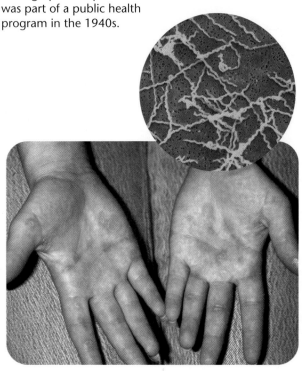

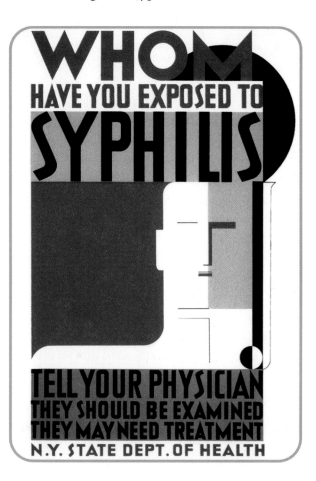

WHOM HAVE YOU EXPOSED TO SYPHILIS

TELL YOUR PHYSICIAN THEY SHOULD BE EXAMINED THEY MAY NEED TREATMENT N.Y. STATE DEPT. OF HEALTH

Seeking Treatment

Being tested for STIs may be uncomfortable and embarrassing, but it is crucial for long-term health. **People who participate in high-risk behaviors should get medical checkups every six months. Individuals who suspect they may be infected should seek prompt medical attention.**

A person who suspects an STI infection should refrain from sexual activity and see a doctor. Depending on the symptoms, the doctor may need to do a physical exam or a blood test. If an infection is present and treatable, the person should start treatment immediately. It is important to finish all of the prescribed medicine, even if symptoms disappear.

If a person finds out that he or she has an STI, it is also important to notify any sexual partners, so they can seek treatment as well. If the STI is not curable, the doctor can offer advice about how to live with the disease and how to prevent passing it on to others.

Many states have clinics that test for STIs. The results of these tests are confidential. Information about clinics that test for STIs is available from state or local public health departments or from the Centers for Disease Control and Prevention.

Doctors keep their patients' information confidential.

FIGURE 8 It is very important for long-term health to see a doctor if you think you might have an STI.

Section 2 Review

Key Ideas and Vocabulary

1. What are three of the most common STIs in the United States? What type of pathogen causes each STI?

2. Why is **pelvic inflammatory disease** a serious problem in women?

3. List the symptoms of hepatitis, gonorrhea, genital herpes, and syphilis.

4. Which stage of syphilis is characterized by the appearance of a **chancre**?

5. When should a person seek treatment for STIs?

Health at Home

Accessing STI Information Write down a list of questions that you have about STIs. Set up a time with a parent or other trusted adult to discuss your questions. If the person doesn't know the answers, ask for his or her help in finding the answers. **WRITING**

Critical Thinking

6. Classifying Which of the STIs that you learned about in this section can be treated but not cured? Which can be cured if treated early?

7. Applying Concepts Suppose a friend is worried about a possible STI. Write an e-mail to your friend, offering your advice about what to do. **WRITING**

HIV and AIDS

Objectives

▶ **Explain** how HIV infection leads to AIDS.

▶ **Describe** how HIV is transmitted from person to person.

▶ **Summarize** the state of HIV infection and AIDS throughout the world.

Vocabulary

- HIV
- AIDS
- asymptomatic stage
- opportunistic infection

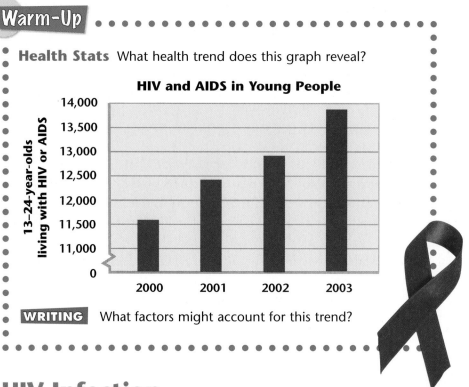

Warm-Up

Health Stats What health trend does this graph reveal?

HIV and AIDS in Young People

13–24-year-olds living with HIV or AIDS

14,000
13,500
13,000
12,500
12,000
11,500
11,000
0

2000 2001 2002 2003

WRITING What factors might account for this trend?

HIV Infection

The most serious incurable STI is caused by the human immunodeficiency virus, commonly called **HIV.** As of 2004, 1 million Americans were reported to be living with HIV. And 13- to 24-year-olds account for approximately 13% of HIV cases reported in the United States.

HIV infection can lead to **AIDS,** or acquired immunodeficiency syndrome, which is an often fatal disease of the immune system. **HIV attacks specific cells of the immune system, disabling the body's defenses against other pathogens. When the immune system becomes severely disabled, the infected person has AIDS.**

How HIV Attacks the Immune System   Inside the body, HIV infects helper T cells, which stimulate other cells of the immune system to produce antibodies against invading pathogens. Inside a helper T cell, HIV reproduces, killing the cell in the process. The new viruses are released from the cell and move on to destroy other helper T cells.

By counting the number of helper T cells that remain active in the body, the progression of HIV infection can be monitored. The fewer helper T cells, the more advanced the disease. Figure 9 shows how helper T cell counts can be used to monitor the progression of the disease.

Stages of HIV Infection
HIV slowly destroys the immune system. Doctors describe HIV infection as progressing through three stages.

▶ **Asymptomatic Stage** Soon after exposure to HIV, an infected person may experience flulike symptoms, which usually go away after a few weeks. Many months or years may follow during which the person shows no outward signs of disease. Because of the lack of symptoms, this period is called the **asymptomatic stage.** During this stage, the virus destroys helper T cells. People in the asymptomatic stage can infect others even though they feel fine.

▶ **Symptomatic Stage** When an HIV-infected person starts to experience symptoms, he or she has entered the symptomatic stage of infection. Symptoms may include weight loss, a persistent fever, diarrhea, or fungal infections. Such symptoms may not appear until 7 to 10 years after infection with HIV.

▶ **AIDS** The onset of AIDS is usually marked by a very low number of helper T cells in the blood, as shown in Figure 9. At this stage, HIV-infected people are usually experiencing even more severe symptoms than in the symptomatic stage. Because the body's ability to fight disease has been weakened by HIV, they are susceptible to infections that a healthy person's immune system could easily fight off.

 Connect to YOUR LIFE Can you assume that someone who looks healthy is not infected with HIV? Explain.

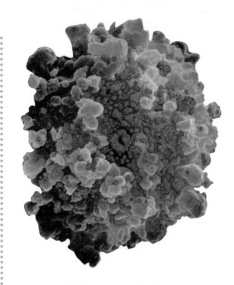

▲ **HIV viruses (red) emerging from a human helper T cell**

FIGURE 9 The number of helper T cells in the blood decreases as HIV infects and destroys more cells. **Reading Graphs** Describe how T cell counts change over time in a person infected with HIV.

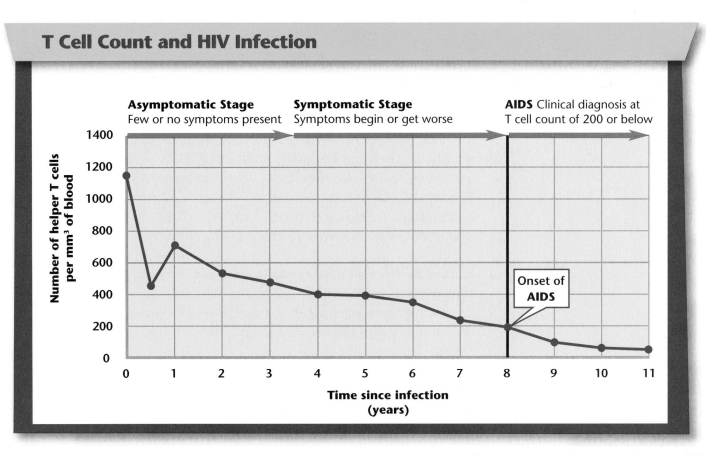

T Cell Count and HIV Infection

Asymptomatic Stage
Few or no symptoms present

Symptomatic Stage
Symptoms begin or get worse

AIDS Clinical diagnosis at T cell count of 200 or below

Number of helper T cells per mm³ of blood

Onset of **AIDS**

Time since infection (years)

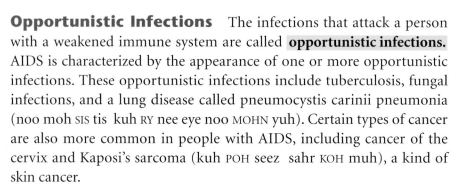

Hands-On Activity

How Quickly Can HIV Spread?

Materials

cups
chocolate candies
cinnamon candies

Try This

1. Your teacher will give you a cup filled with small candies. Do not look inside the cup.
2. Walk around the room until your teacher tells you to stop. At that point, pair up with the student closest to you.
3. Pour a few of the candies from your cup into your partner's cup. Your partner should also pour some candies into your cup.
4. Repeat steps 2 and 3 two more times.
5. Look at the candies in your cup. If you have a cinnamon candy, you have been "infected" with HIV.

Think and Discuss

1. How many people in your class ended up with a cinnamon candy (HIV) in their cup? Would it surprise you to learn that only one person was infected to begin with?
2. Suppose that each person you exchanged candies with represents a sexual partner. How many people other than you did each of your partners exchange candies with? What does this suggest about having multiple sexual partners and the chances of getting infected with HIV or another STI?

Opportunistic Infections   The infections that attack a person with a weakened immune system are called **opportunistic infections.** AIDS is characterized by the appearance of one or more opportunistic infections. These opportunistic infections include tuberculosis, fungal infections, and a lung disease called pneumocystis carinii pneumonia (noo moh SIS tis kuh RY nee eye noo MOHN yuh). Certain types of cancer are also more common in people with AIDS, including cancer of the cervix and Kaposi's sarcoma (kuh POH seez sahr KOH muh), a kind of skin cancer.

People living with AIDS often experience severe weight loss. As the disease progresses, the virus may attack the brain and nervous system, causing blindness, depression, and mental deterioration. Death is usually caused by an opportunistic infection.

Connect to YOUR LIFE   Would you spend time with a friend who is HIV-positive if you were sick with the flu? Explain.

Transmission of HIV

People with HIV are infectious whether or not they have any symptoms of disease. **Individuals infected with HIV can pass the virus on to someone else through the exchange of blood, semen, vaginal secretions, or breast milk.**

Risky Behaviors   There are four main ways that HIV spreads from person to person.

▶ **Sexual Contact** HIV can be transmitted through any form of sexual contact that involves contact with an infected person's body fluids, including vaginal, oral, and anal sex. Infected fluids can enter a person's bloodstream through sores or tiny cuts in the lining of the mouth, vagina, rectum, or opening of the penis.

▶ **Shared Needles** HIV can be transmitted through shared needles or syringes that are contaminated with the blood of an infected person. Therefore, sharing needles for tattoos or body piercings and injecting illegal drugs put you at risk for HIV infection.

▶ **Contact With Blood** HIV can be transmitted if a person has an open cut or sore that comes into contact with the blood or blood parts of an infected person. Avoid all contact with others' blood.

▶ **Mother to Baby** HIV can pass from an infected mother to her child, either during pregnancy, birth, or breast-feeding. Certain drugs can decrease the chances of transmission during pregnancy, and the doctor might deliver the baby by cesarean section to reduce the risk of transmission during birth. In addition, mothers infected with HIV should not breast-feed their babies.

Go Online
HEALTH LINKS

For: Updates on AIDS
Visit: www.SciLinks.org/health
Web Code: ctn-7223

FIGURE 10 It is safer for an HIV-positive mother to bottle-feed, rather than breast-feed, her baby.

In the United States, mother-to-child transmission of HIV has decreased dramatically in recent years.

FIGURE 11 Playing contact sports such as rugby does not put you at risk for HIV infection.

FIGURE 12 The global distribution of HIV infections is uneven. **Sequencing** List the areas of the world from greatest number of infected people to smallest number of infected people. What position does North America have on the list?

Safe Behaviors HIV is not transmitted by casual contact. You cannot get HIV by going to classes or eating lunch with an infected person. You cannot get HIV by holding hands or hugging an infected person. Families who live with an infected person are not at risk of contracting HIV unless they engage in high-risk behaviors. Small amounts of HIV occur in saliva, tears, and perspiration. However, the amounts are so small that infection from contact with these fluids is unlikely.

The Safety of Donated Blood The risk of getting HIV from blood transfusions is extremely small. Since 1985, all of the blood collected in the United States has been tested for the presence of HIV. Blood that tests positive for HIV antibodies is discarded. Potential donors are interviewed and are not allowed to give blood if they have engaged in behaviors that place them at risk for HIV infection.

A Global Problem

Figure 12 shows the global distribution of HIV infections. **With approximately 40 million people infected around the world, HIV and AIDS represent a global health problem.**

▶ **Africa** Sub-Saharan Africa accounts for more than half of all global infections. Some estimates indicate that, if infections continue to rise at the current rate, 80 million Africans may die from AIDS by 2025.

▶ **Asia** HIV infections are also increasing in certain parts of Asia. For example, researchers estimate that over 5 million people are living with HIV and AIDS in India.

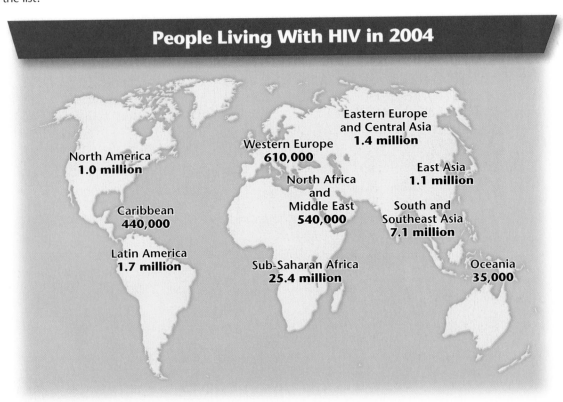

People Living With HIV in 2004

North America
1.0 million

Caribbean
440,000

Latin America
1.7 million

Western Europe
610,000

Eastern Europe
and Central Asia
1.4 million

North Africa
and
Middle East
540,000

Sub-Saharan Africa
25.4 million

East Asia
1.1 million

South and
Southeast Asia
7.1 million

Oceania
35,000

High-Risk Groups In all areas of the world, HIV is spreading among people who share needles to inject drugs and people who engage in high-risk sexual behaviors. In many countries, young women represent the majority of new HIV infections. In sub-Saharan Africa, for example, 75% of young people infected with HIV are female. The higher infection rates in women are often due to a lack of information about how to protect themselves or, in some cases, a lack of power to protect themselves.

Education and Prevention Several international organizations are working to lessen the toll that HIV and AIDS are taking on populations all over the world. The World Health Organization and the Joint United Nations Programme on HIV/AIDS monitor the situation and recommend steps for stemming the epidemic in different countries.

The main goal of international organizations is HIV education. Making people in high-risk countries aware of how to protect themselves from HIV infection is a huge step toward prevention. Because treatment can be very expensive and inaccessible for the people at highest risk, much effort is put toward preventing HIV infection in the first place.

In addition to prevention education, international organizations coordinate treatment efforts for people already living with HIV and AIDS. Efforts are being made to provide medicine to millions of infected people in countries most affected by HIV and AIDS.

FIGURE 13 A girl from Zambia, a country in Africa, holds a sign she made for World AIDS Day.

Section 3 Review

Key Ideas and Vocabulary

1. Explain how HIV affects the immune system and how it eventually leads to AIDS.

2. What is meant by an **opportunistic infection**? Give an example.

3. What are four ways that HIV can be transmitted from an infected person to an uninfected person? List three ways HIV is *not* transmitted.

4. Which region of the world accounts for the majority of HIV infections?

Critical Thinking

5. Making Judgments Should teens in the United States be concerned about the global AIDS problem? Why or why not?

Health at School

AIDS Awareness Plan an AIDS Awareness Day at your school. Divide your class into groups to make posters about different aspects of HIV and AIDS. For example, one poster could focus on how HIV is transmitted. Another poster could focus on the status of the AIDS epidemic. Display your posters at school to help educate other students. WRITING

6. Evaluating HIV is more common in poorer countries than in wealthier countries. Why do you think this might be the case?

Protecting Yourself From HIV and AIDS

Objectives

▶ **Identify** three behaviors that can prevent the spread of HIV.

▶ **Describe** how a person gets tested for HIV.

▶ **Describe** the goal of HIV treatment.

Vocabulary

• universal precautions
• HIV-positive
• viral load

Warm-Up

Dear Advice Line,

Lately my boyfriend has been asking me to have sex. I really like him, but I'm not ready for that. Plus I'm not sure he's telling me everything about his past. What should I do?

WRITING Write a response to this teen, encouraging her to choose abstinence. What would you tell her about the risk of becoming infected with HIV and other STIs?

Preventing HIV Infection

At present there is no cure for HIV or AIDS. But, the good news is that you can choose behaviors that will help you avoid this very serious disease. **You can protect yourself from HIV by practicing abstinence, avoiding drugs, and avoiding contact with others' blood and body fluids.**

Practice Abstinence As with other STIs, the best way to avoid HIV and AIDS is sexual abstinence. Sexual activity such as oral sex, anal sex, genital-to-genital touching, and intercourse can transmit HIV. It is much easier to be abstinent if you choose friends who have also decided to be abstinent. Going out with groups of responsible friends can reduce the pressure you may feel to engage in sexual behavior.

Avoid Drugs Avoiding drug use is also extremely important for reducing the risk of HIV infection. People who share contaminated needles to inject themselves with drugs are at a high risk for contracting HIV. People who have sex with drug abusers are also at high risk. Do not inject illegal drugs, and avoid sexual contact with anyone who uses illegal drugs.

Using alcohol or other drugs can impair a person's judgment. People with impaired judgment are more likely to engage in behaviors that place them at risk. To guard against infection, you need to be able to think clearly so you can make healthy decisions.

Connect to YOUR LIFE How can your choice of friends help you avoid risky behaviors?

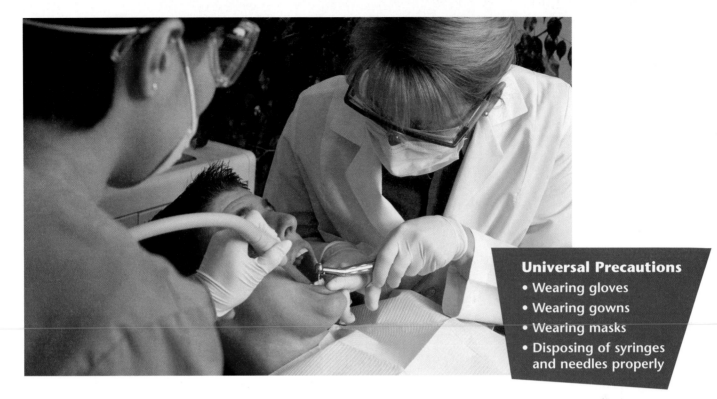

Universal Precautions
- Wearing gloves
- Wearing gowns
- Wearing masks
- Disposing of syringes and needles properly

Avoid Contact With Blood or Body Fluids Never share any personal items that may have blood or other body fluids on them. For example, razors, toothbrushes, syringes, and piercing or tattoo needles should never be shared. In addition, mothers who are infected with HIV should not breast-feed their babies because the virus can be transmitted through breast milk.

Healthcare providers often come into contact with the blood and body fluids of patients. To reduce the risk of HIV transmission, doctors, nurses, dentists, dental hygienists, and other healthcare providers practice **universal precautions,** as listed in Figure 14.

Sexual Fidelity in Marriage If two people are uninfected with HIV at the start of a long-term monogamous relationship such as marriage, sexual fidelity by both partners will protect them from HIV. However, if either partner has practiced risky behaviors in the past, he or she should be tested for HIV and other STIs. Teens should *not* count on sexual fidelity to protect them from HIV.

Barrier Protection For people who are sexually active, but not in a long-term monogamous relationship, the best way to reduce their risk of HIV infection is to use a condom every time they engage in sexual activity. The condom must be made out of latex or polyurethane, be free of tears, and be used in accordance with the directions on the package. Condoms serve as a physical barrier against HIV and some of the pathogens that cause STIs. When used consistently and correctly, condoms are highly effective in preventing the spread of HIV. However, condoms are not 100% effective. Abstinence remains the best protection against HIV and other STIs.

FIGURE 14 Healthcare providers protect themselves and their patients by following universal precautions.

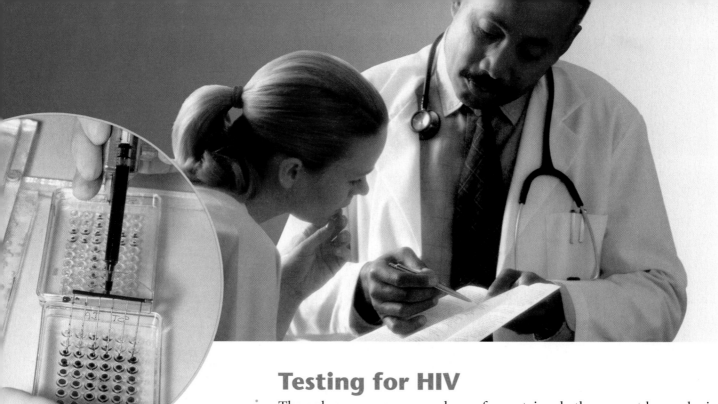

FIGURE 15 A blood test can reveal if a person is infected with HIV. Getting an HIV-positive result can be frightening and depressing. Therefore, it is important that HIV-positive individuals receive counseling to help them deal with the emotional impacts of their infection.

Testing for HIV

The only way a person can know for certain whether or not he or she is infected with HIV is to have a blood test. People who engage in risky behaviors should have their blood tested at a clinic or by a private physician. The names of clinics that provide confidential HIV testing are available from each state's department of public health or from the Centers for Disease Control and Prevention. People who think they may have been exposed to HIV should practice abstinence to avoid spreading the virus.

In an HIV test, a person's blood is tested for antibodies to HIV. If antibodies are detected, a second test is done to verify the result. A person who is diagnosed as being infected with HIV is said to be **HIV-positive.**

An HIV-Positive Diagnosis If a person is diagnosed as HIV-positive, he or she needs to notify all previous sexual partners so that they can also be tested. Early diagnosis is important to prevent the spread of the disease and to start treatment as soon as possible.

It is difficult to cope with an HIV-positive diagnosis. For this reason, it is recommended that individuals receive counseling from a healthcare professional before being tested. People who learn they are HIV-positive should receive additional counseling.

Reasons for Follow-Up Testing If an HIV infection is recent, a blood test may not be accurate. This is because there is a lapse between the time of infection and the time when antibodies show up in a person's blood. Antibodies usually show up within three months after infection. So even if no antibodies are detected in the person's first blood test, he or she should avoid all high-risk behaviors and be tested again in three months.

Connect to YOUR LIFE How could you convince someone of the importance of follow-up testing?

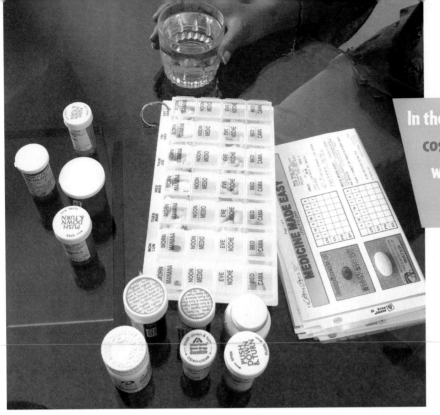

In the United States, medical costs for a person living with HIV may be over $30,000 a year.

FIGURE 16 A common treatment regimen requires an HIV-positive person to take many pills each day. If the person misses too many doses, the virus may develop resistance to the medication.

Treatment for HIV and AIDS

Although there is no cure for HIV infection and AIDS, some treatments can add many years to a patient's life. The sooner a person begins treatment, the more effective it can be in slowing the progress of the disease.

The Goal of Treatment **The main goal of HIV treatment is to keep the person's immune system functioning as close to normal as possible.** To achieve this goal, the treatment must

▶ keep the person's **viral load**—the number of virus particles circulating in the body—as low as possible, and

▶ keep the person's T cell count as high as possible.

If both of these goals are achieved, the patient's immune system is more capable of fighting off opportunistic infections. Remember that current treatments do not rid the body of HIV. They try to stop HIV from destroying the immune system.

Combination Drug Therapy The most common treatment for HIV infection today is known as Highly Active AntiRetroviral Therapy, or HAART. HAART uses a combination of drugs to reduce the viral load in the blood. Multiple drugs are necessary to prevent the virus from reproducing inside helper T cells. A doctor prescribes a combination of drugs that is right for each individual patient.

Some drawbacks to HAART are its complicated dosage schedules, its cost, and its side effects, which can include liver and kidney damage. Furthermore, if a person is not consistent about taking the drugs exactly as prescribed, drug resistance can develop quickly.

Go Online
PHSchool.com

For: More on HIV/AIDS prevention
Visit: PHSchool.com
Web Code: ctd-7224

Living With HIV People who are HIV-positive must take extra care to practice healthful behaviors. Eating right, exercising, and getting plenty of sleep are especially important for people who are HIV-positive. Regular visits to the doctor are also important for monitoring a patient's health and the effectiveness of HIV treatment.

When they are healthy, HIV-positive people can carry on with their careers and other activities. But they do have to avoid high-risk behaviors that put them at risk for infecting someone else. And because HIV compromises the immune system, they should stay away from anyone who has an infectious disease.

The Need for Support As with any serious disease, people who are HIV-positive as well as their loved ones need a lot of support to help them deal with their distress and anxiety. Support may include counseling, healthcare services, and financial assistance.

HIV-positive individuals should be treated with compassion. They also should be allowed to live their lives with dignity. Because HIV cannot be transmitted by casual contact, such as hugging or shaking hands, no one needs to be fearful of working or going to school with someone who is HIV-positive.

FIGURE 17 Every year, thousands of people participate in walks to help raise money for AIDS research and education.

Section 4 Review

Key Ideas and Vocabulary

1. What are three behaviors that can help you avoid HIV infection?

2. What does an HIV test involve?

3. What does **HIV-positive** mean?

4. What is the main goal of HIV treatment? How is that goal achieved?

Critical Thinking

5. Evaluating Depression can be a serious problem in people who are HIV-positive. What do you think are some ways to help people deal with the mental and emotional effects of this disease?

Health at School

HIV Prevention Some schools introduce HIV prevention education in grades six to eight. Find out if you or a group of classmates could prepare a program to help educate these younger students about protecting themselves from HIV infection. Then, develop an outline for your program. **WRITING**

6. Relating Cause and Effect Doctors recommend that people who are HIV-positive should stay as healthy as possible, eating well, getting enough sleep, and avoiding exposure to anyone with an infectious disease. Why do doctors recommend this?

Chapter 5

Review

Discovery EDUCATION TEENS Talk

Risks and STIs List three things you learned from the video about the importance of sexual abstinence.

Reviewing Key Ideas

Section 1

1. Being unable to have children is
   a. STI.
   b. epidemic.
   c. infertility.
   d. abstinence.

2. How can teens best avoid STIs?

3. List four kinds of sexual activity that can transmit STIs.

4. **Critical Thinking** If you found out that the person you were dating had injected illegal drugs in the past, how would that affect your relationship?

Section 2

5. A serious infection of the female reproductive organs that can be caused by chlamydia is
   a. pelvic inflammatory disease.
   b. genital warts.
   c. syphilis.
   d. trichomoniasis.

6. An STI that *cannot* be treated with antibiotics is
   a. gonorrhea.
   b. chlamydia.
   c. human papilloma virus.
   d. syphilis.

7. How can genital herpes affect a newborn baby?

8. What steps should be taken by a person who suspects that he or she is infected with an STI?

9. **Critical Thinking** Why should someone who is diagnosed with an STI notify all of his or her sexual partners?

Section 3

10. The virus that causes AIDS is
    a. herpes.
    b. HPV.
    c. PID.
    d. HIV.

11. HIV destroys
    a. neurons.
    b. antibodies.
    c. B cells.
    d. T cells.

12. Why do people with AIDS fall victim to opportunistic infections?

13. Describe four ways that HIV is spread.

14. **Critical Thinking** Jason has engaged in high-risk sexual behavior, but he feels fine. He sees no reason to get tested for HIV or any other STI. What would you tell Jason about the importance of getting tested?

Section 4

15. Which of these behaviors is *not* a way to protect yourself from HIV?
    a. avoiding contact with blood
    b. practicing abstinence
    c. sharing needles
    d. avoiding alcohol

16. HIV-positive people receive treatments to keep
    a. their viral load as high as possible.
    b. their viral load as low as possible.
    c. their viral load equal to their T cell count.
    d. their T cell count as low as possible.

17. In what ways can HIV treatment be difficult?

18. **Critical Thinking** Alyssa has engaged in high-risk sexual behavior in the past three months. She had an HIV test a month ago that came back negative. Should she be tested again? Explain.

19. **Critical Thinking** Experts consider education critical in preventing HIV infection. Do you agree? Explain your answer.

Building Health Skills

20. **Analyzing Influences** Do the media do a good job in educating people about HIV and other STIs? Give examples to support your answer.

21. **Advocacy** What could teens do to make abstinence an easier choice for their peers?

22. **Setting Goals** List some goals you have for the next ten years. How could practicing abstinence now help you achieve those goals? **WRITING**

Health and Community

Public Service Announcement Some people behave in sexually risky ways. In many cases, they don't get tested regularly for HIV or other STIs. Create a public service announcement that emphasizes the risks of certain behaviors and the importance of getting tested. Indicate where people in your community can go to get tested for HIV and other STIs. **WRITING**

A

abstinence The act of refraining from, or not having, sex. (p. 46)
abstinencia Acción de privarse de tener relaciones sexuales.

adolescence The period from about age 12 to 19 during which a child gradually changes into an adult. (p. 9)
adolescencia Período entre los 12 y los 19 años aproximadamente, durante el cual un(a) niño(a) se convierte gradualmente en adulto.

AIDS Acquired immunodeficiency syndrome, an often fatal disease of the immune system caused by HIV infection. (p. 98)
SIDA Sigla del síndrome de inmunodeficiencia adquirida, una enfermedad del sistema inmunológico, por lo general fatal, causada por el virus de inmunodeficiencia humana (VIH).

amniocentesis A prenatal test in which a small amount of amniotic fluid is removed and tested for abnormalities. (p. 71)
amniocentesis Examen prenatal que consiste en extraer una pequeña cantidad de líquido amniótico y someterlo a pruebas para detectar anormalidades.

amniotic sac A fluid-filled bag of thin tissue that develops around the embryo. (p. 66)
saco amniótico Bolsa de tejido fino, llena de líquido, que se forma alrededor del feto.

asymptomatic stage The stage of HIV infection in which the infected person shows no symptoms. (p. 99)
etapa asintomática Etapa de la infección del VIH durante la cual la persona infectada no muestra síntomas.

B

bisexual A person who is sexually attracted to people of both sexes. (p. 13)
bisexual Persona que siente atracción sexual por gente de ambos sexos.

blastocyst A hollow, spherical structure made up of about 50 to 100 cells that attaches to the uterus during implantation. (p. 65)
blastocisto Estructura hueca de forma esférica, con aproximadamente 50 a 100 células, que se adhiere al útero durante la implatación.

body image The way a person sees his or her physical self. (p. 12)
imagen corporal La manera en que una persona se ve a sí misma físicamente.

C

chancre A painless sore that appears during the first stage of syphilis infection. (p. 96)
chancro Llaga indolora que aparece en la primera etapa de la sífilis.

chlamydia A very common sexually transmitted infection caused by bacteria. (p. 93)
linfogranuloma venéreo Infección de transmisión sexual muy común, causada por una bacteria.

chorionic villus sampling A prenatal test in which a piece of the developing placenta is removed and tested for inherited disorders. (p. 71)
muestra de vellosidad coriónica Prueba prenatal que consiste en sacar un fragmento de la placenta y examinarlo para detectar trastornos hereditarios.

commitment A strong determination to make a marriage a fulfilling, lifelong relationship. (p. 61)
compromiso Fuerte determinación para hacer de un matrimonio una relación satisfactoria y de por vida.

compatibility The ability of particular people to live together in harmony. (p. 61)
compatibilidad Capacidad de cierta gente para vivir junta y en armonía.

compromise An agreement in which each party gives up something. (p. 61)
concesión Acuerdo por el cual cada participante cede algo.

contraception or birth control The use of any accepted method to intentionally prevent pregnancy. (p. 77)
contracepción o control de la natalidad Uso de cualquier métado aceptado para prevenir el embarazo.

cystitis An infection of the urinary bladder. (p. 34)
cistitis Infección de la vejiga urinaria.

D

date rape A rape that occurs during a date. (p. 51)
violación en una cita Violación que ocurre en el transcurso de una cita.

dating violence A pattern of physical, emotional, or sexual abuse that occurs in a dating relationship. (p. 49)
violencia en el noviazgo Patrón de maltrato físico, emocional, o sexual que se presenta entre dos personas que son novios.

E

ectopic pregnancy A condition resulting from the implantation of the blastocyst in a location in the abdomen other than the uterus. (p. 72)
embarazo ectópico Condición causada por la implantación del blastocisto en una zona del abdomen que no sea el útero.

effectiveness In reference to a contraceptive method, the likelihood that using that method will prevent pregnancy. (p. 77)
efectividad En referencia a un método contraceptivo, la posibilidad de que el uso de un método prevenga el embarazo.

ejaculation The ejection of semen from the penis. (p. 22)
eyaculación Eyección del semen por el pene.

embryo The stage of human development from the two-cell stage until about nine weeks after fertilization. (p. 65)
embrión Etapa del desarrollo humano que tiene lugar a partir de la división del cigoto en dos células hasta aproximadamente la novena semana después de la fecundación.

emotional abuse The nonphysical mistreatment of a person. (p. 49)
maltrato emocional Todo maltrato que no sea de índole físico.

emotional intimacy The openness, sharing, affection, and trust that can develop in a close relationship. (p. 46)
intimidad emocional Franqueza, comunicación intensa, afecto y confianza que se desarrollan en una relación íntima.

erection The state in which the penis becomes larger and stiffer as chambers in it become filled with blood. (p. 22)
erección Estado en el que el pene crece y se endurece a medida que los cuerpos cavernosos del pene se llenan de sangre.

estrogen The female sex hormone that signals certain physical changes at puberty and controls the maturation of eggs. (p. 27)
estrógeno Hormona sexual femenina que regula ciertos cambios físicos durante la pubertad, así como la maduración de los óvulos.

F

failure rate In reference to a contraceptive method, the percentage of women who become pregnant while using that method for one year. (p. 77)
tasa de fracasos En referencia a un método contraceptivo, el porcentaje de mujeres que quedan embarazadas mientras usan ese método específico durante un año.

fallopian tubes The passageways that carry eggs from the ovaries to the uterus. (p. 28)
trompas de Falopio Tubos que transportan los óvulos desde los ovarios al útero.

fertilization The process of a sperm cell joining with an egg. (p. 20)
fecundación Proceso mediante el cual un espermatozoide se une con un óvulo.

fetus The stage of human development from the third month after fertilization until birth. (p. 67)
feto Etapa del desarrollo humano que tiene lugar a partir del tercer mes después de la fecundación hasta el nacimiento.

G

gender roles The behaviors and attitudes that are socially accepted as either masculine or feminine. (p. 5)
papeles sexuales Conductas y actitudes que son socialmente aceptadas como masculinas o femeninas.

gender The way people perceive maleness or femaleness to be defined by society. (p. 4)
género La manera en que la gente percibe la masculinidad o femineidad para ser definidos por la sociedad.

genital herpes A sexually transmitted infection caused by the herpes simplex virus. (p. 95)
herpes genital Infección de transmisión sexual causada por el virus del herpes simple.

gestational diabetes Diabetes that develops during pregnancy. (p. 72)
diabetes gestacional Diabetes que se desarrolla durante el embarazo.

gonorrhea A bacterial sexually transmitted infection that infects the urinary tract of males and females and the reproductive organs of females. (p. 94)
gonorrea Infección bacterial de transmisión sexual que infecta las vías urinarias del hombre y los órganos reproductores de la mujer.

H

heterosexual A person who is sexually attracted to members of the opposite sex. (p. 13)
heterosexual Persona que se siente atraída sexualmente por personas del sexo opuesto.

HIV The human immunodeficiency virus, an incurable sexually transmitted infection that can lead to AIDS. (p. 98)
VIH Virus de inmunodeficiencia humana, una infección de transmisión sexual incurable que puede producir el SIDA.

HIV-positive A person who is diagnosed as being infected with HIV. (p. 106)
VIH-positivo Persona que se diagnostica como infectada con el VIH.

homosexual A person who is sexually attracted to members of the same sex. (p. 13)
homosexual Persona que se siente atraída sexualmente por personas del mismo sexo.

human papilloma virus A very common viral sexually transmitted infection. (p. 93)
virus del papiloma humano Infección viral de transmisión sexual muy común.

hymen A thin membrane that may partly cover the vaginal opening. (p. 29)
himen Delgada membrana que cubre parcialmente la abertura vaginal.

I

implantation The process in which the blastocyst attaches itself to the wall of the uterus. (p. 65)
implantación Proceso mediante el cual el blastocisto se adhiere a la pared del útero.

incest Sex between people who are too closely related to marry legally. (p. 52)
incesto Relación sexual entre personas de parentesco demasiado cercano como para poder casarse legalmente.

infatuation Feelings of intense attraction to another person. (p. 40)
enamoramiento Sentimiento de atracción intensa hacia otra persona.

infertility The condition of being unable to reproduce. (p. 26)
infertilidad Incapacidad para reproducirse.

M

mammogram An X-ray of the breast that may detect breast cancer. (p. 36)
mamografía Radiografía de la mama que permite detectar el cáncer de mama.

masturbation The touching of one's own genitals for sexual pleasure. (p. 23)
masturbación Tocarse los genitales propios para obtener placer sexual.

menopause The time of life during which the ovaries slow down their hormone production and no longer release mature eggs. (p. 31)
menopausia Período de la vida en el que los ovarios disminuyen su producción de hormonas y dejan de liberar óvulos maduros.

menstrual cycle The process during which an ovary releases a mature egg that travels to the uterus; if the egg is not fertilized, the uterine lining is shed and a new cycle begins. (p. 31)
ciclo menstrual Proceso mediante el cual el ovario libera un óvulo maduro que se dirige hacia el útero; si el óvulo no es fecundado, la capa uterina interna es expulsada y comienza un nuevo ciclo.

miscarriage The death of an embryo or fetus in the first 20 weeks of pregnancy. (p. 72)
aborto espontáneo Muerte de un embrión o feto en las primeras 20 semanas del embarazo.

monogamy A term describing a sexual relationship in which two people have sexual contact only with each other; also called sexual fidelity. (p. 91)
monogamia Término que describe una relación sexual en la cual dos personas tienen contacto sexual sólo entre ellas; también llamada fidelidad sexual.

N

nocturnal emission An ejaculation during sleep. Also called a "wet dream." (p. 23)
emisión nocturna Eyaculación durante el sueño. También llamado "sueño húmedo".

O

obstetrician A doctor who specializes in pregnancy and childbirth. (p. 70)
obstetra Médico que se especializa en el embarazo y el parto.

opportunistic infection An infection that attacks a person with a weakened immune system. (p. 100)
infección oportunista Infección que ataca a una persona que tiene debilitado el sistema inmunológico.

orgasm Sexual climax, marked by ejaculation in males and rhythmic contractions of the muscles of the vagina and pelvis in females. (p. 22)
orgasmo Clímax sexual, marcado por la eyaculación en los hombres y contracciones rítmicas de los músculos de la vagina y la pelvis en las mujeres.

ova The reproductive cells in females. (p. 27)
óvulos Células reproductoras femeninas.

ovaries The female reproductive glands. (p. 27)
ovarios Glándulas reproductoras femeninas.

ovulation The process during which one of the ovaries releases a ripened egg. (p. 27)
ovulación Proceso durante el cual un ovario libera un óvulo maduro.

Pap smear A medical procedure in which a sample of cells is taken from the cervix and examined under a microscope. (p. 36)
Prueba de Papanicolaou Procedimiento médico en que se toma una muestra de células del cuello uterino y se examinan bajo microscopio.

pedophilia A mental disorder in which a person has a sexual attraction to children. (p. 52)
pedofilia Trastorno mental en el que una persona siente atracción sexual por los niños.

pelvic inflammatory disease A serious infection of the female reproductive organs that can lead to infertility or an ectopic pregnancy. (p. 93)
enfermedad inflamatoria pélvica Infección grave de los órganos reproductores femeninos, que puede conducir a la infertilidad o al embarazo ectópico.

penis The external male sexual organ through which sperm leave the body. (p. 21)
pene Órgano sexual externo masculino a través del cual el cuerpo libera semen.

physical abuse Intentionally causing physical harm to another person. (p. 49)
maltrato físico Daño físico que se causa a otra persona de manera intencional.

placenta A structure that lines the wall of the uterus during pregnancy and nourishes the embryo or fetus with substances from the mother's blood. (p. 66)
placenta Estructura que recubre las paredes de útero durante el embarazo y alimenta al embrión o feto con sustancias de la sangre de la madre.

pornography Images and words that are designed to excite sexual arousal. (p. 56)
pornografía Imágenes y palabras destinadas a provocar excitación sexual.

preeclampsia A serious condition during pregnancy characterized by high blood pressure, swelling of the wrists and ankles, and high levels of protein in the urine. (p. 72)
preclampsia Trastorno serio del embarazo que se caracteriza por hipertensión arterial, inflamación de las muñecas y los tobillos, y la presencia de niveles elevados de proteínas en la orina.

prenatal care Medical care received during pregnancy. (p. 70)
cuidados prenatales Atención médica recibida durante el embarazo.

progesterone A hormone that signals changes to a woman's reproductive system during the menstrual cycle and pregnancy. (p. 27)
progesterona Hormona que regula los cambios del sistema reproductor de la mujer durante el ciclo menstrual y el embarazo.

prostitution When one person pays to have sex with another person. (p. 56)
prostitución Cuando una persona paga por tener relaciones sexuales con otra persona.

puberty The period of sexual development during which a person becomes sexually mature and physically able to reproduce. (p. 9)
pubertad Período de desarrollo sexual durante el cual la persona madura sexualmente y es capaz de reproducirse.

rape A type of assault in which one person forces another to have sexual relations. (p. 51)
violación Tipo de asalto en el cual una persona fuerza a otra a tener relaciones sexuales.

reproductive maturity The ability to produce children, signaled by the onset of ovulation in girls, and of sperm production in boys. (p. 10)
madurez reproductiva Capacidad de procrear, indicada por el comienzo de la ovulación en las niñas y la producción de espermatozoides en los niños.

scrotum A sac of skin that contains the testes. (p. 20)
escroto Bolsa de piel que contiene los testículos.

secondary sex characteristics Physical changes during puberty that are not directly involved in reproduction. (p. 10)
caracteres sexuales secundarios Cambios físicos que ocurren durante la pubertad y que no están directamente relacionados con la reproducción.

self-concept What a person thinks of himself or herself, physically and mentally. (p. 12)
autoconciencia Lo que una persona piensa de sí misma, tanto física como mentalmente.

semen The mixture of sperm and fluids produced by the glands of the male reproductive system. (p. 22)
semen Mezcla de espermatozoides y fluidos producidos por las glándulas del sistema reproductor masculino.

sexual abuse Forcing a person to engage in any unwanted sexual behavior. Includes rape and any use of a child by an adult for sexual purposes. (p. 49)
abuso sexual Forzar a una persona a mantener cualquier comportamiento sexual no deseado. Incluye violación y cualquier tipo de uso de un niño por parte de un adulto con propósitos sexuales.

sexual awakening The increased awareness of and sexual attraction to other people that begins around the time of puberty. (p. 13)
despertar sexual Aumento de la conciencia y de la atracción sexual hacia otras personas, que comienza alrededor de la época de la pubertad.

sexual harassment Any uninvited and unwelcome sexual remark or sexual advance. (p. 53)
acoso sexual Todo comentario o acción de carácter sexual que es mal recibido por una persona.

sexuality Everything that relates to, reflects, or expresses a person's maleness or femaleness. (p. 4)
sexualidad Todo lo relacionado, que refleja o expresa la femineidad o masculinidad de una persona.

sexually transmitted infection (STI) An infection caused by any pathogen that spreads from one person to another during sexual contact. (p. 88)
infección de transmisión sexual (ITS) Infección causada por cualquier patógeno que se transmite de una persona a otra por contacto sexual.

sperm The reproductive cells in males. (p. 20)
espermatozoides Células reproductoras masculinas.

spermicide A chemical agent that kills sperm. (p. 78)
espermicida Agente químico que mata los espermatozoides.

statutory rape Having sex with someone who is under the age of consent. (p. 51)
estupro Tener relaciones sexuales con una persona menor de la edad de consentimiento para tener relaciones sexuales.

sterilization The use of surgery or other procedure to make a person incapable of reproduction. (p. 81)
esterilización Uso de cirugía u otro procedimiento para hacer a una persona incapaz de reproducirse.

syphilis A serious bacterial sexually transmitted infection that progresses through three distinct stages. (p. 96)
sífilis Enfermedad bacterial grave de transmisión sexual que se desarrolla en tres etapas distintas.

testes The male reproductive glands. (p. 20)
testículos Glándulas reproductoras masculinas.

testicular torsion The twisting of a testis so that the blood vessels leading to the testis also twist, cutting off the blood supply. Testicular torsion is an emergency that requires immediate medical attention. (p. 24)
torsión testicular Retorcimiento de un testículo de modo que los vasos sanguíneos que llevan sangre al testículo también se retuercen, cortándose el flujo sanguíneo. La torsión testicular es una emergencia que requiere atención médica inmediata.

testosterone The sex hormone that affects the production of sperm and signals certain physical changes at puberty. (p. 20)
testosterona Hormona sexual que determina la producción de espermatozoides y regula ciertos cambios físicos durante la pubertad.

trichomoniasis A sexually transmitted infection caused by a protozoan that infects the urinary tract or vagina. (p. 92)
tricomoniasis Infección de transmisión sexual causada por un protozoo que infecta las vías urinarias o la vagina.

trimester One of three periods of time that divide a pregnancy. Each trimester is approximately three months long. (p. 70)
trimestre Cada uno de los tres períodos en los que se divide el embarazo. Cada trimestre dura aproximadamente tres meses.

U

ultrasound High-frequency sound waves used to create an image of a developing fetus. (p. 71)
ultrasonido Ondas sonoras de alta frecuencia utilizadas para crear una imagen del feto en desarrollo.

umbilical cord The cordlike structure that connects the embryo or fetus and the placenta. (p. 67)
cordón umbilical Estructura en forma de cuerda que conecta al embrión o feto con la placenta.

universal precautions Actions taken by healthcare providers that reduce their risk of coming into contact with blood and body fluids. (p. 105)
precauciones universales Medidas que toman los profesionales de la salud para reducir el riesgo de entrar en contacto con la sangre y otros fluidos corporales.

urethritis Inflammation of the lining of the urethra. (p. 92)
uretritis Inflamación del revestimiento interno de la uretra.

uterus The hollow, muscular, pear-shaped organ in which a fertilized egg develops and grows. (p. 28)
útero Órgano muscular hueco, en forma de pera, en el cual se desarrolla y crece el óvulo fecundado.

V

vagina The hollow, muscular passage leading from the uterus to the outside of the female body. (p. 28)
vagina Canal muscular que comunica el útero con el exterior del cuerpo femenino.

vaginitis A vaginal infection or irritation. (p. 34)
vaginitis Infección o irritación de la vagina.

values The standards and beliefs that are most important to you and that help you decide what is right and wrong. (p. 14)
valores Normas y creencias que son muy importantes para ti, y que te ayudan a decidir lo que es bueno y malo.

viral load The number of virus particles circulating in the body. (p. 107)
carga viral Cantidad de partículas de un virus que circulan en el cuerpo.

Z

zygote The united egg and sperm. (p. 65)
cigoto Óvulo y espermatozoide ya unidos.

Acknowledgments

Note: Every effort has been made to locate the copyright owner of material reprinted in this book. Omissions brought to our attention will be corrected in subsequent editions.

Staff Credits

The people who made up the **Prentice Hall Health** team—representing design services, editorial, editorial services, education technology, market research, marketing services, planning and budgeting, product planning, production services, publishing processes, and rights and permissions—are listed below. Boldface type denotes the core team members.

Jennifer Angel, Alan Asarch, **Amy C. Austin,** Charlene Barr, Peggy Bliss, Stephanie Bradley, **Jim Brady, Diane Braff, Sarah G. Jensen,** Linda D. Johnson, **James Lonergan, Dotti Marshall, Natania Mlawer,** Julia F. Osborne, **Paul M. Ramos, Nancy Smith,** Amanda M. Watters

Additional Credits AARTPACK, Inc., Dan Breslin, Laura J. Chadwick, Liz Good, Russ Lappa, Ellen Levinger, Brent McKenzie, Laurel Smith, Emily Soltanoff, Linda B. Thornhill

Illustration

Young Sook Cho: 25, 35; **John Edwards, Inc.:** 21, 22, 32, 28-29, 65, 66, 81. **All additional art created by AARTPACK, Inc.**

Photography

Photo Research AARTPACK, Inc.

Cover tl (faucet) G. Bliss/Masterfile; (water) Getty Images, Inc.; **tm** Getty Images, Inc.; **tr** Siede Preis/Getty Images, Inc.; **ml** Getty Images, Inc.; **mm** Getty Images, Inc.; **mr** Rebecca Bradley/Getty Images, Inc.; **bl** Chris Everard/Getty Images, Inc.; **bm** (traffic lights) Mark Wiens/Masterfile; (clouds) Photodisc/Getty Images, Inc.; **br** Getty Images, Inc.

Table of Contents Page iv t, David Young-Wolff/PhotoEdit; **iv br,** Comstock Images/Age Fotostock; **iv bl,** BananaStock/Jupiter Images; **1 t,** Hemera Technologies/Alamy; **1 bl,** Syracuse Newspapers/Suzanne Dunn/The Image Works; **1 br,** Thinkstock/Jupiter Images.

Chapter 1 Pages 2–3, Peter Langone/ImageState; **4,** Bananastock/Fotosearch; **5 b,** Thomas Tolstrup/Getty Images; **5 m,** Wang Leng/Getty Images; **5 t,** Bananastock/Fotosearch; **6,** Creasource/Corbis; **7,** Steve Smith/Getty Images; **8,** Nico Kai/Getty Images; **9,** David Young-Wolff/PhotoEdit; **10 l,** Richard Haynes; **10 r,** Comstock/PictureQuest; **12 l,** Michael Newman/PhotoEdit; **12 m,** Stockbyte/SuperStock; **12 r,** Tom & Dee Ann McCarthy/Corbis; **14,** David Young-Wolff/PhotoEdit; **15,** SW Productions/Getty Images; **16,** Comstock Images/Age Fotostock.

Photography *(continued)*

Chapter 2 Pages 18-19, Stewart Cohen/Getty Images; **20,** Joel Sartore/Getty Images; **22,** Phototake Inc./Almay; **23,** Bananastock/Fotosearch; **24,** Syracuse Newspapers/Suzanne Dunn/The Image Works; **25,** David Young-Wolff/PhotoEdit; **26,** Patrick Ramsey/ImageState; **27,** SW Productions/Getty Images; **30,** Andersen Ross/Getty Images; **31,** RubberBall Productions/Imagestate; **33,** Thinkstock/Jupiter Images; **34,** Pixland/AgeFotostock; **35,** Will Ryan/Corbis; **36,** Pete Saloutos/Corbis.

Chapter 3 Pages 38-39, Michael Pole/Corbis; **40,** BananaStock/Jupiter Images; **41,** Chuck Savage/Corbis; **42,** Paramount/The Kobal Collection; **45,** Janine Wiedel Photolibrary/Alamy; **46,** Loretta Ray/Getty Images; **47,** KK/Central Park Zoo, NYC; **48,** SW Productions/Getty Images; **49,** Jeff Greenberg/Age Fotostock; **50,** Brad Wilson/Getty Images; **52,** Enough Abuse Campaign/Massachusetts Citizens for Children; **54,** Comstock/SuperStock; **56,** Richard Heinzen/SuperStock.

Chapter 4 Pages 58-59, Spencer Grant/Photo Researchers, Inc.; **60,** Ingram Image/PictureQuest; **61,** Ziggy Kaluzny-Charles Thatcher/Getty Images; **62,** Nick Dolding/Getty Images; **63,** Trinette Reed/PictureQuest; **64 r,** Michael Newman/PhotoEdit; **64 l,** Yorgos Nikas/Getty Images; **67 b,** Petit Format/Photo Researchers, Inc.; **67 t,** Claude Edelmann/Photo Researchers, Inc.; **68,** Siede Preis/Getty Images; **68,** Photodisc/Fotosearch; **69,** Plush Studios/PictureQuest; **70 l,** Thinkstock/Fotosearch; **70 r,** Bananastock/PictureQuest; **71,** Gary Bistram/Getty Images; **72,** Knut Mueller/Peter Arnold, Inc.; **73,** David Young-Wolff/PhotoEdit; **74,** Richard Haynes; **76,** Spencer Grant/PhotoEdit; **77,** Rubberball/Getty Images; **78 t,** White Packert/Getty Images; **78 b,** Keith Brofsky/Getty Images; **79 l,** Michael Newman/PhotoEdit; **79 m,** Michael Newman/PhotoEdit; **79 r,** Cervical Barrier Advancement Society; **80 t,** Ray Ellis/Photo Researchers, Inc.; **80 m,** Canadian Press/Phototake; **80 b,** Custom Medical Stock Photo; **83,** Royalty Free/Corbis; **84,** Supershoot Images/Getty Images.

Chapter 5 Pages 86-87, Cindy Charles/PhotoEdit; **88,** BananaStock/SuperStock; **89,** Bob Daemmrich/The Image Works; **90 b,** Brand X Pictures/Fotosearch; **90 t,** Will Hart/PhotoEdit; **91,** Roy Morsch/Zefa/Corbis; **92,** David Young-Wolff/PhotoEdit; **93 l,** Eye of Science/Photo Researchers, Inc.; **93 m,** Custom Medical Stock Photo; **93 r,** Alfred Pasieka/Photo Researchers, Inc.; **94 b,** SIU/Peter Arnold, Inc.; **94 t,** Alfred Pasieka/Photo Researchers, Inc.; **95 t,** David M. Phillips/Photo Researchers, Inc.; **95 b,** Eye of Science/Photo Researchers, Inc.; **96 tl,** Dr. Kari Lounatmaa/Photo Researchers, Inc.; **96 bl,** Logical Images/Custom Medical Stock Photo; **96 r,** Library of Congress, Prints and Photographs Division, LC-USZC2-944; **97,** Royalty Free/Corbis; **98,** Hemera Technologies/Alamy; **99,** NIBSC/Photo Researchers, Inc.; **100 t,** John Rich; **100 b,** John Rich; **101,** Royalty Free/Corbis; **102,** David Young-Wolff/PhotoEdit; **103,** Sean Sprague/The Image Works; **104,** E Dygas/Getty Images; **105,** Royalty Free/Corbis; **106 r,** Jose Luis Pelaez, Inc./Corbis; **106 l,** Klaus Guldbrandsen/Photo Researchers, Inc.; **107,** Michael Newman/PhotoEdit; **108,** AP/World Wide Photos.